*Dedicated to Ava Rosabelle Close,
who, at the tender age of ten months,
already has a great laugh.*

*My thanks to Dustin Stinett, Looy Simonoff,
Jeff Welch, Jeff Haas, Jamy Ian Swiss, and
especially Stephen Minch. Their keen eyes greatly
improved the quality of this book.*

*Thanks to Paul Stone for his encouragement
and enthusiasm for this project.*

*And a warm thank you to the many people who have
brought me laughter through the years. You have a
special place in my heart.*

Contents

Foreword by Penn Jillette	1
Introduction	5
About This Book	7
Dad	11
Indiana	25
Michael B.	43
Vegas	61
Jay	77
Eric	95
Aldo	109
Billy	123
Chuck	141
Bob	165
James B.	175
Last Laugh	207

Foreword

By Penn Jillette

When you get to the joke in this book with the punchline ". . . breakfast was my idea," try to remember that that punch should be " . . . the pie was my idea." Remember that. "The pie was my idea." Read that sentence aloud. Feel it roll off your tongue. It's a little like saying "Lolita," isn't it? "The pie was my idea": the tip of the tongue taking a funny little trip from the light comedy voiceless bilabial plosive of "Pie," leading into the internal rhyme - "The **pie** was **my**" and then the assonance of "Idea." All the while keeping up the six iambic feet ending with an unaccented syllable. Now that's a fucking punchline! Hey, Close, "Breakfast" has no comedic business being in that joke. Or, maybe I just like pie.

Yes, Close and I can quibble, and you can bet your ass we will. (How did he do "A" instead of "G" for the first note the bass player plays in the band doing their last show before the big break? Both "A" and "G" are fine pop keys, but if you use "G" then you can show your bravery by almost tipping the punch by having all the other band members start their musings with "Gee." That's the way a big swinging dick tells it.) See, we can quibble.

We can quibble because Close knows jokes. When Close and I are hanging, we really try to talk about our kids. We do. We try to care. We also try to talk about professional magic stuff. You know, we're dads, husbands, and magicians. Close and I work together, and we could talk about the tricks we're working on and shit. We should have lots of other stuff to talk about besides jokes. Maybe his kid is sick? I should ask him about his daughter. I mean he even does a chapter on his daughter in this joke book. The reason he got around to writing this book was he was stuck in Guatemala forfuckingever adopting that little bundle of joy. I should ask him about beautiful Ava. He's my friend and he loves her and I love my kids, and we should really ask each other about the kids, but . . . you know, I just heard this joke I've been waiting to tell Close . . . so fuck the kids. ("Do we have time?" the priest asks.)

I love talking jokes with Close and this book is just that. One joke reminds him of another and off we go. The best thing you could do is hang out with Close and tell jokes all night when you should be talking about your kids. But, second best is this book. You'll have fun. And, if you tell these jokes, just the way he tells you to tell them (with the few little changes mentioned above, and, yeah, I have a few more little changes if you and I are ever really talking jokes), you'll be a funny guy. No shit. Really. These jokes will work for you. I've known Close since I told him the "Big Orange Head" joke and he took credit for it at a magic convention, the rat bastard. I've known him a long time, and even after all these years, I'd never heard the "Cross-eyed Beagle" joke until I read it in this book and that got me laughing aloud in the bathtub and that usually takes at least a good unexpected bubble.

Okay, so I'll talk about the kids. Several hours before Mox, our first baby, was born, we were all hanging out at Starbucks waiting for the time to go the hospital. My mother-in-law, Diane, Close's wife, Lisa, my wife, EZ and I were all sitting enjoying our beverages. The women folk were talking about birthing babies. Close and I were talking jokes. EZ's contractions started. Every several minutes, EZ, would groan in pain. Diane was holding her hand and timing the contractions. Like a good grandmother-to-be, she was announcing how far apart they were. We were in single digits. It was almost time to go to the hospital. Soon, our beautiful first child would be born. But, there was something else going on. Diane would announce that EZ was at 3:25 second intervals and Close would think of a joke he could tell in that exact amount of time. Close would tell the joke and right on the punchline, EZ would double over in pain and we would all laugh. That's the kind of guys we are.

But, even if you're not that kind of guy – you'll still love this book.

Remember, "The pie was my idea."

Introduction

From the age of seventeen I have made my living from music and magic, and in both fields I have held a variety of jobs. As a musician I have been a cocktail pianist, led a jazz trio, accompanied lounge-lizard singers, played in a country-western band, taught at the college level, written jingles and industrial post-score music, and (as a recording session keyboardist) spent hundreds of hours in the studio playing on projects as diverse as custom gospel albums to full-blown orchestral sessions (such as the tracks for the *Disney on Ice* shows). As a magician, I have performed close-up magic in restaurants, bars, cocktail parties, and hospitality suites. I have done stand-up magic, and I've served as a master of ceremonies for big, full-evening magic shows. I've created original magic routines, and have lectured on this material for magicians around the world. I've written many books and ebooks. For more than a decade I have served as a product reviewer for the two major independent magic magazines.

I have received varying degrees of personal satisfaction from all these jobs, but the thing that I enjoy the most isn't to be found in the previous paragraph. I like to make people laugh. Nothing makes me happier than to hear a group of people roaring with laughter at a joke I've told. My magic performances are full of humor, but joke telling, for the most part, is my avocation – I've never tried to make a living as a stand-up comedian. I tell jokes informally, usually in a small group situation, often trading jokes back and forth with someone else in the group. It is particularly enjoyable if one of the participating joke tellers has a couple of stories I haven't heard before, because I enjoy laughing at a well-told joke as much as I enjoy being the joke teller.

At the end of one of these joke-telling sessions, I'm invariably asked by a listener, "How in the world do you remember all of those jokes?" The answer is that I remember jokes by association; one joke reminds me of another, which reminds me of another, and so forth. Many times the association is thematic, such as a blonde joke reminding me of another blonde joke. But I often form more complex associations, relating jokes through their construction, or the nature of their punch lines. Through these associations, I can retrieve jokes that I hadn't thought about in years.

In high school and college, especially during the years that I worked on my music degrees, I was the go-to guy for jokes. When someone passed a new joke on to me, I would retell it to my circle of acquaintances, which in my music school days was composed of thirty to forty people. Telling the joke that many times really locked it into my memory, and I could easily retrieve my mental storehouse of jokes. Nowadays, I encounter fewer people during the course of a day, so if I hear a new joke I may only retell it three or four times. Consequently, it is often easier for me to recall a joke I heard thirty years ago than one I heard yesterday. Even though I try to construct associations whenever I hear a joke, I fear that some very funny ones have just slipped away. (Although the good news is that as I typed the previous sentence I thought of three very funny Alzheimer's jokes.) Anyway, it seems that now would be a very good time to record the jokes that I have told throughout my life, and to set them down through the associations that allow me to recall them – a stream of consciousness joke book, if you will. This process should dredge up a lot of jokes that I thought I had forgotten, and recording them for posterity will be good for me and good for all the people who have asked me over the years, "Do you have all those jokes written down somewhere?"

In addition to the jokes, I also wanted to pay tribute to the funny people who have enriched my life. Often, I associate a joke with when and where I heard it, and who told it to me. If you are a magician, many of these people will be familiar to you; others will be unfamiliar. All of them have made me laugh, and for that I am forever in their debt.

But before you jump into the jokes, be sure to read the next chapter, which has important information.

About This Book

This is not a collection of every joke I've ever heard. Nor did I surf the Internet, gathering all the jokes I could find just to publish a book. The jokes in this book are jokes with which I've had a personal relationship. These are jokes that I have told and retold for many years (some for more than forty years). These are the best jokes I know; they are fun to tell, and they will get big laughs.

Good joke telling demands acting skills: inflection, intensity, pacing, enthusiasm, and timing. I can't teach you any of those things. If you don't have these skills, you'll need to learn and practice them. Listening to good joke tellers will help a lot. One of the biggest mistakes that novice joke tellers make is to add extraneous information. Long jokes are great (and there are plenty of them in this book), but all the details offered have to be crucial to the surprise of the punch line. I have written the jokes exactly the way I tell them, in the way that works for me. You should, of course, adapt the jokes to fit your way of speaking, but I would advise against altering them too much.

One critical aspect of joke telling is sizing up an audience, delivering material that is appropriate to the group. When I work for larger groups of people, I always keep the material squeaky clean. I may, after a few jokes, drop in a joke that is slightly risqué. If I get an enthusiastic response to that joke, I may push the envelope a little further. If I sense discomfort at the risqué joke, I may drop back into the squeaky clean realm. My point is that it is unfair to make an audience listen to material and language that they were not expecting. If people go to a comedy club, they have an expectation of the type of jokes they will hear. (Although even in Las Vegas, at the Improv in Harrah's, there is a sign warning patrons of the adult level of the material.) People who encounter me in a hospitality suite, or in the Close-up Gallery of the Magic Castle, or in a corporate stand-up magic show are not expecting raunchy material. They might enjoy those kinds of jokes, but I'm going to start clean and let them guide me to where they want the show to be.

I'll give you a real-life example. A few years ago I was the Master of Ceremonies for the big gala show at a magic convention in England. I had done this type of work before, but only for American conventions. Different countries have different sensibilities. I had a legal pad full of jokes, but I needed a way to test the waters, to find out quickly what types of jokes were going to work. So, I took a chance. The producer of the show was a man named John Pye. To me, John epitomizes the look of the dignified English gentleman. His wife is equally charming. Here's the joke I did.

> I'm from Las Vegas, which is hot and dry, and I've spent the week here in Southport, which is cold and damp. This morning the weather caught up with me and I woke up with a terrible case of laryngitis. I tried gargling with salt water, drank hot tea with lemon and honey, but nothing worked. I was very afraid that I would not be able to perform on the show tonight. I thought that I should warn John Pye that he might have to find a replacement for me. I called his room in the hotel. His wife answered the phone. I said [in a very hoarse whisper], "Hi, this is Mike Close. Is John there?" She said [also whispering], "No. Come on up."

The joke got a huge laugh, and I knew the type of material that would work. Even so, as the show progressed I constantly changed and updated the jokes on my legal pad.

> "A limerick packs laughs astronomical
> Into space that is quite economical.
> But the good ones we've seen
> So seldom are clean
> And the clean ones so seldom are comical."

As I sit here at the computer, I have no way of knowing what your taste in jokes is. I love clean jokes, and I love making an audience laugh using nothing but clean jokes. I'm happy to say that this book contains a large number of really funny clean jokes. You could tell these jokes to your mother, and she would love you for it. (And as the limerick so succinctly points out, it's not easy to find a great clean joke.)

However, I'm not a prude; I also love to hear (and tell) dirty jokes as well. The jokes in this collection that aren't squeaky clean fall somewhere between the PG-13 and R-rated categories. Either the theme is more adult in nature, or the joke contains one of those words that you can't say on network television, but which are now rather commonplace on cable TV. My initial organizational plan was to keep the clean jokes and the more risqué jokes separated. That turned out to be impractical, as it destroyed the flow of the book. Consequently, you'll find clean and "less clean" jokes mixed together. The overtly sexual dirty jokes have been relegated to the back of the book, in the chapter titled James B. Read the introduction to that chapter and decide what you want to do.

Let me say one more thing about language. If words that are not normally used in polite company bother you, you should probably put this book down and read something else. You will find such words sprinkled throughout the book. I did not use these words cavalierly. I use language carefully, especially when I tell jokes. The right word can make or break a joke. Sometimes, the right word is a vulgar word. Jokes are funny because of the surprise of the punch line. Sometimes that surprise is intensified by the use of a "shock" word. The joke needs the shock value of that word. However, overusing such words lessens their effectiveness; they lose their shock value. As you read through this book, you can be assured that I have thoughtfully considered the words I used.

Some of the jokes in this collection rely on visual punch lines. These jokes play great in the telling, but not so great in the reading. Rather than have you get into a joke and then be disappointed when the punch line is visual, I have placed an eyeball symbol in the margin next to the joke. For these jokes I have described the visual actions required in brackets (like the "whispering" cue in the John Pye joke above).

Happy reading.

Dad

My father's parents were Polish Jews who came to the United States at the beginning of the 20th century. When they hit Ellis Island, their last name, Klos, was Anglicized to "Close," an event that, seventy years later, had significant repercussions for me when I began specializing in close-up magic. The following conversation has occurred many times.

> Random Magician/Spectator: Is Close your real last name?
> Me: No, it's really Hitler, but I changed it because I couldn't get any work.

My last name has also caused some confusion. Here's how a magician attempted to introduce me to another magician. (I am not making this up; it really happened.)

> Magician: And this is Michael Klause.
> Me: Close.
> Magician: Krause?

Humor was a big part of my father's family life, but it was humor used as a defense mechanism. Around the dinner table the zingers came fast and furious, and if you weren't quick with a comeback you were eaten alive. My aunts, uncles, and cousins lived in Toledo, Ohio, and during family visits I quickly discovered how the attack/defense dynamic worked, learning how to take it, as well as how to dish it out. Over the years I honed my wit to rapier sharpness, and used it to devastating effect; unless you were prepared to bring the big guns, you didn't want to get into a verbal battle with me. I came to realize, however, that this was a lousy approach to personal interaction (whether it was with an audience or in daily encounters), so I now avoid it. As Elwood P. Dowd said in *Harvey*, "I've been smart, and I've been nice. I'd rather be nice."

My father, who died in April of 2007, didn't talk a lot. We had a relationship based on love and respect, but not a lot of conversation. I knew almost nothing about his childhood, college years, or his life as a mechanical engineer (and later as a Professor of Mechanical Engineering Technology at the Purdue University Extension campus in Indianapolis). I knew that he was a guy who occasionally did funny things. I remember, for example, that when I was ten years old I bought an Egg Bag (a trick in which an egg vanishes and reappears inside a plain cloth bag) at Stoner's Magic Shop. It came with a realistic wooden egg. At that time, we were living in Fort Wayne, Indiana, and my father was working in Lebanon, Indiana, which was about two hours away. On Monday mornings, my father would get up very early to drive to Lebanon, where he would spend the week, coming back home Friday night. I bought the Egg Bag on a Saturday. The following Sunday night, Dad slipped the wooden egg into the refrigerator, just so he could secretly watch my mother beat the crap out of the kitchen counter as she tried to break that egg, attempting to make his (very) early Monday morning breakfast.

I did not think of my father as someone who told a lot of jokes, or who made funny, situational comments. But I was wrong. I discovered this side of Dad's humor in 1997, when my parents celebrated their 50th wedding anniversary. At the ceremony/reception I made some comments about my parents, several of which were pretty funny. Afterward, people came up to me and said, "You're definitely Sam's son, you have his sense of humor. You sound just like him." I sound like him? Who knew? Not me, that's for sure.

I mention all this about my father because I do have a vivid memory of him telling me a joke, a joke that I thought was absolutely hysterical. As well as I can remember, it was the only joke he ever told me. I was probably thirteen at the time. It's a Polish joke, and since I'm half Polish, I think it is a good joke to start off this collection. The joke goes like this.

 Two Polish fellows are digging a ditch. They are hot, sweaty, and covered in dirt, and as they labor another man stands above them, telling them what to do. One of the ditch diggers says to the other, "Why are we down here digging, and he's up there bossing us around?"

"I don't know," says the other.

"Well, go up there and find out why."

So, the Polish fellow climbs out of the ditch and walks up to the foreman. "Why are we down there digging and you're up here bossing us around?" he asks.

"Intelligence," replies the foreman.

"Intelligence? What's that?"

"Here, I'll show you," says the foreman. He places his right hand against a tree trunk. "Hit my hand with your shovel."

"I can't do that; I'll break your hand."

"It's all right. Go ahead. Hit my hand as hard as you can with your shovel."

So, the Pole pulls back, and with all his might swings his shovel at the foreman's hand. At the last instant, the foreman pulls his hand away, and the shovel smacks into the tree trunk.

"See," says the foreman, "that's intelligence. Now, get back down in that ditch and keep digging."

The Polish fellow climbs back into the ditch and resumes his work. His friend asks, "So, why are we doing all the work and he's up there bossing us around?"

"Intelligence."

"Intelligence? What's that?"

"I'll show you." The Pole looks around, and then puts his hand in front of his face. "Here, hit my hand as hard as you can with your shovel."

[Obviously, when you tell this joke you won't say the words, "and then puts his hand in front of his face." You'll simply put *your* hand in front of *your* face as you say, "Here, hit my hand as hard as you can with your shovel." Many of the jokes in this book end with visual punch lines, and I will describe what you'll need to do when you tell them. This means, of course, that the jokes won't be hilarious to read, but I guarantee that you'll get big laughs when you tell them.]

And that reminds me:

A fellow walks into a bar in the Loop in Chicago. He sits at the bar and orders a beer. As the bartender serves him, the fellow says, "Hey, would you like to hear a Polack joke?"

The bartender, a large, beefy guy, replies, "Before you tell that joke, you should know that I'm Polish. You see the two guys sitting to your left, the guys who look like they could be steel workers? They *are* steel workers, and they're both Polish. You see the two guys sitting to your right, the guys who look like they're offensive linemen for the Chicago Bears? They *are* offensive linemen for the Bears, and they are both Polish. Now, do you really want to tell that joke?"

"Hell no," says the man. "I don't want to have to explain it five times."

*

An Englishman, a Frenchman, and a Pole are trying to sneak into the Summer Olympic Games. The Englishman comes up with an idea. "We'll pretend we're athletes, and the guard at the gate will let us in."

So saying, the Englishman grabs a broom, breaks off the handle, strips down to his underwear, and runs up to the guard. "England – javelin," he announces. The guard lets him in. The Frenchman grabs a manhole cover, strips down to his underwear, runs up to the guard, and says, "France – discus." The guard lets him in.

The Pole looks around, grabs a hunk of barbed wire,

strips down to his underwear, runs up to the guard, and announces, "Poland – fencing!"

*

A Polish fellow wants to fight in World War I. He makes his way to France, eventually coming upon an air force base. He explains that he wants to fight for the cause, so he is given some basic flight training.

After several weeks of training he is allowed to go up for his first solo flight. He's flying over the French countryside, enjoying the view, when all of sudden, from out of the sun, comes Baron Von Richthofen, the Red Baron. The Baron starts firing, and the poor Pole tries every maneuver he can think of to get away, but nothing works. The Baron closes in, and just when it seems as if death is imminent, the Polish fellow sneezes, falls forward on the control stick, goes into an impossibly tight inner loop, and ends up behind the Baron. He pulls the trigger of his machine gun, and shoots the Baron down.

The Pole returns to his base, reports the incident, and the French troops find Richthofen, who has survived the crash. They bring the Baron back to the base hospital. A few days later, the Polish fellow visits him.

"I feel bad about shooting you down," the Pole says. "It was really an accident. By all rights, you should have shot me down. Is there anything I can do for you?"

"Yes, there is something," replies the Baron. "The doctors tell me that my right leg is so severely damaged that it has to be amputated. After they cut it off, will you take it up in your plane, fly it over Germany, and throw it back into the Fatherland?"

The Polish fellow agrees, and the next day, after the surgery, he takes the leg up in his plane, flies over Germany, and throws it out into the countryside. A week later, he visits the Baron again.

"Is there anything else I can do for you?" he asks.

"Yes, there is. The doctors are going to remove my right arm tomorrow. It cannot be repaired. Will you throw my arm back into Germany, back into the Fatherland?"

"Sure, I'd be glad to do that," replies the Pole, and the next day he takes the arm up in his plane and throws it back into the German countryside.

Several weeks pass before the Pole has a chance to visit the Baron again. Unfortunately, the German's wounds have not improved, and he is fading quickly. The Baron can only muster enough strength to open one eye. He sees the Polish fellow.

"Will you do me another favor?" he asks weakly. "Sure," replies the Pole. "My other leg has developed gangrene, and tomorrow they will cut it off. Will you return it to the Fatherland for me?"

"Absolutely," says the Polish fellow. "But, listen. Be honest with me. You're not trying to escape, are you?"

[This is a long joke, and I try to maintain interest by making my telling of it as dramatic as possible. I do a German accent when I speak the Baron's lines, and I emphasize his deteriorating condition by reducing his voice to a hoarse whisper.]

*

A shepherd is tending to his flock when a stranger walks up to him.

"Are you a gambling man?" asks the stranger. "Yes, I am," replies the shepherd. "In that case, I have a little wager for you," says the stranger. "If I can guess how many sheep there are, you give me $100 and my pick of the flock." "I'll take that bet," says the shepherd.

The stranger looks over the flock for a moment. "There are exactly 186 sheep here," he announces. "That's absolutely correct," exclaims the shepherd. "How could you possibly know?" "That's not important," says the stranger. "Just give me my $100 and let me get my animal."

> The shepherd hands over the money and the stranger picks up one of the flock and starts to leave. "Wait a minute," says the shepherd. "I have a bet for you. If I can tell you your nationality, I get my hundred dollars and my animal back." "I'll take that bet," says the stranger.
>
> "You're Polish," says the shepherd. "That's absolutely correct," says the stranger. "How could you possibly know?"
>
> "That's not important," says the shepherd. "Just give me back my money and put down my dog."

Even though it's off the subject, that joke reminds me of this one.

> A man has a beagle that he has owned for several years. One day he notices that the beagle has become cross-eyed. He takes the dog to the vet. The vet picks up the dog and carefully looks at the dog's eyes. Then he checks the dog's teeth and looks in his ears.
>
> "I'm going have to put this dog down," he announces. "My god," says the owner, "just because he's cross-eyed?" "No," says the vet, "because he's really heavy."

Back to subject at hand.

> Two Polish fellows are walking along the railroad tracks. They come upon a pair of severed legs. "My gosh," says one, "those look like Joe's legs." "They are Joe's legs," says the other.
>
> As the two continue along the tracks they see a severed pair of arms. "Hey," says one, "those look like Joe's arms." "They are Joe's arms," says the other.
>
> A few minutes later they see a severed torso. "I think this is Joe's torso." "It is Joe's torso."
>
> They finally come upon a head lying by the tracks. "That looks like Joe's head." The other man picks up the head. "It is Joe's head." He shakes the head. "Hey, Joe! You okay?"

[One of the great things about collecting jokes is discovering two jokes that have almost exactly the same set-up but that have different punch lines. (You'll find several more of these later in the book.) The previous joke is an example, because there is an alternate punch line. Follow the above set-up until the Polish fellows find the severed torso. Then continue thusly:]

After walking a bit farther, they see a head lying by the tracks. One of the men picks up the head, holding it by the hair. "Hey, I think this is Joe's head!" "No," the other replies, "he wasn't that tall."

*

Stash Kowalski has lived his entire life in a Polish neighborhood in Chicago. He's sick and tired of being the butt of Polish jokes, so he decides to reinvent himself. He changes his name to Aldo Colombini and moves to an Italian neighborhood, where he decorates his house with pictures of the Coliseum, the Leaning Tower of Pisa, and other Italian landmarks. He hangs a small Italian flag on his front porch. Looking through his cupboards, he realizes that he has to get rid of all his Polish food and restock his larder with Italian food. So he goes to the store.

"I want a pound each of prosciutto, mortadella, mascarpone, caciocavallo, and parmigiano. I also need two loaves of focaccia bread, some fresh olives, and some extra virgin olive oil."

"You're Polish, aren't you?" says the clerk.

"How could you possibly know that?"

"This is a hardware store."

And that reminds me of this.

A blonde walks into a library. She says to the librarian, "I'd like a Big Mac, a small order of fries, and a strawberry milk shake."

The librarian says, "This is a library."

The blonde says, "Oh, I'm so sorry. [Whispered voice] I'd like a Big Mac, a small order of fries, and a strawberry shake."

Back to the Polish jokes:

During World War II, a young man wants to join the fight, so he hooks up with a Polish resistance group. The soldiers are preparing for a major engagement with the Germans. A sergeant is handing out rifles to the soldiers, but the young man doesn't get a rifle.

"Sergeant," he says, "I didn't get a rifle." "No problem," says the sergeant, handing the young man a broom. "When the fighting starts, just point this and say, 'Bangity, bangity, bang.'"

The sergeant hands out bayonets, and the young man doesn't get one. "Sergeant," he says, "I didn't get a bayonet." "No problem," says the sergeant, and he ties a piece of straw to the end of the broom handle. "When the fighting starts, just poke this at the enemy and say, 'Stabity, stabity, stab.'"

The sergeant hands out hand grenades, and – guess what – the young man doesn't get one. "Sergeant," he yells, "I didn't get a hand grenade." "No problem," says the sergeant, and he gives the young man a couple of apples. "When the fighting starts, pull the stem out, throw the apple, and say, 'Boomity, boomity, boom.'"

Later that day, the Polish resistance unit encounters the Germans in a fierce battle. The young man points his broom and yells, "Bangity, bangity, bang." He pokes his broom and yells, "Stabity, stabity, stab." He pulls the stem from an apple, throws it, and yells, "Boomity, boomity, boom."

The smoke clears, and the young man looks around. All around him are dead soldiers. Only one other man remains standing on the battlefield, a German soldier who is walking straight toward him. The young man points his broom and yells, "Bangity, bangity, bang," but the German soldier keeps approaching. He pokes his broom and yells, "Stabity, stabity, stab," but the soldier keeps coming. He pulls the stem from another apple, throws it, and yells, "Boomity, boomity, boom."

The soldier keeps coming. He walks right over the young man, trampling him into the mud. Just before he expires, he hears the German soldier saying, "Tankity, tankity, tank. Tankity, tankity, tank."

*

Kowalski gets a job working 9 to 5 as a janitor in a factory, sweeping up the main factory floor. At 3 p.m. one afternoon, the foreman comes up to him. "I'm leaving early," he says, "but I want you to keep cleaning until 5." Kowalski does so.

This situation occurs several times during the week. One day, after the foreman has left early, one of Kowalski's friends says to him, "Hey, the foreman is gone. Why don't you go home, too? You can spend a little more time with your wife." Kowalski thinks, "Why not?" and heads home.

Just as he approaches his front door, the door opens, and the foreman comes out of the house. Kowalski dives into the bushes to avoid being seen. The next afternoon, the foreman again announces that he is leaving early. Once he departs, Kowalski's friend asks, "Are you going to skip out early again today?" "Hell, no," he says. "I almost got caught yesterday!"

*

Three friends are trying to decide where to have a drink. "I know a great bar," says Tom. "You buy the first drink, and you buy the second drink, but the third drink is free."

"I know a better place than that," says Bill. "You buy the first drink, but the second drink is free."

"I know a better place than that," says Kowalski. "They buy all the drinks, and at the end of the evening you get laid."

"Wow, that sounds like a terrific bar," says Tom. "How did you hear about it?"

"My wife told me."

*

Two Polish fellows decide to go ice fishing. They haul out all their gear, and one of them starts to drill a hole in the ice. Suddenly, a voice booms out from the heavens, "There are no fish under the ice."

The two guys look around, see no one, and shrug it off. Again they start to drill a hole.

"There are no fish under the ice!"

Again, they look around. There is no one to be seen. They start to drill again.

"**There are no fish under the ice!!**"

The Polish fellows look heavenward. "Who are you?" they cry.

"The arena manager!"

[This is a great joke to do on stage; the use of a microphone (and judiciously applied reverb) makes it very effective. I have also done this as a two-man joke with an off-stage announcer. Very funny.]

The ice fishing scenario of the previous joke reminds me of this one, which Tony Randall told to Johnny Carson on the *Tonight Show*.

Two men are ice fishing on a bitterly cold day. They have been out for hours and haven't caught a single fish. About one hundred feet away from them, a young boy has cut a hole in the ice, and he is pulling out fish after fish. The men are baffled by this, so they walk over to the boy to find out his secret.

"How do you do it?" they ask. "How are you able to catch so many fish?" "Mhhph ghrgd da kpheh uphg wmphng wmphrd," says the boy. "What?" say the men. "Mhhph ghrgd da kpheh uphg wmphng wmphrd," repeats the boy. "We don't understand you," say the men.

The boy spits something into his cupped hands. "You've got to keep your worms warm."

[I never say "The boy spits something into his cupped hands." I mime that action.]

On another appearance on the *Tonight Show,* Randall told the following joke, and he wiped out Carson with it. It is one of my favorites, and I've told it often.

- A man lives in a neighborhood where the mob has a great deal of influence. One day, he pays a visit to the Godfather. "Godfather," he says, "my son is a deaf mute. He graduates from high school in a few days and is unsure what he wants to do next. Is there something he could do in your organization?" The Godfather says, "Sure. He can help run the numbers for me. Have him come by and I'll show him what to do."

  So, for the next year the son runs numbers for the Godfather. At the end of a year the father gets a phone call from the Godfather. "Hey, we just went over the books. Your son is $200,000 short. Bring him here."

  The father and the deaf mute son appear before the Godfather. The Godfather says to the father, "Ask him where the money is." The father signs to his son, "You're in trouble. They went over the books and you're $200,000 short. What did you do with the money?"

  The boy signs back to his father, "Dad, I have no knowledge of this loss. I would never steal from these guys. I don't have the money." The father says to the Godfather, "Godfather, my son knows nothing about this. He would never cheat you."

  The Godfather takes out a gun and sets it on his desk. "Ask him where the money is."

  The father signs to his son, "Listen, this guy is serious. What did you do with the money?" The son signs back, "Dad, I'm innocent. I swear on my mother's grave that I know nothing about this." The father says to the Godfather, "My son swears on his mother's grave that he knows nothing about this."

  The Godfather picks up the gun, cocks it, and puts it against the son's forehead. "Ask him where the money is."

> The father signs to his son, "I'm telling you, this guy is not playing Russian Roulette with you. He's really mad. Where's the money?" The son signs back, "Okay, okay, okay. I took the money. It's in a black duffle bag in the attic."
>
> The father says to the Godfather, "He says, 'Go to hell.'"
>
> [When I tell this joke, I do the Godfather's voice á la Brando. I also mime the signing when the father and son are talking. Feel free to make the last line harsher than it is above. It gives the joke a little more punch.]

But I seem to have gotten a little off track.

> Kowalski gets a job at a lumber mill. His job is to slide large pieces of plywood through a table-saw blade. The foreman shows him what to do and then turns away. He hears Kowalski say, "Ouch."
>
> "What happened?" asks the foreman.
>
> "I don't know," says Kowalski. "I just stuck my hand out like this and...well, shit, there goes the other one."

*

> Kowalski sees an enticing ad in the newspaper – Two Week Cruise to Bermuda Only $79! He goes to the travel agency listed in the ad and purchases the $79 ticket. On the morning of the cruise, he arrives at the dock, walks up the gangplank, and shows his ticket to the steward. The steward looks at the ticket and blows a whistle; suddenly two big burly guys grab Kowalski and drag him below decks, where he is chained to an oar, next to an Armenian fellow.
>
> As the day goes on, the hold of the ship fills up with people who have purchased the $79 cruise ticket. By three o'clock every seat is occupied. A big black man comes in and sits down at a large drum. A man with a whip appears. A heavy "Boom, boom, boom" resonates through the hold as the black man pounds out a cadence. Everyone grabs hold of the oars, and, under the prodding of the man with the whip, the unfortunate passengers row the cruise ship to Bermuda.

The trip takes three and a half days. When the ship docks in Bermuda, the steward comes down to the hold. "We're going to unchain you; you can leave the ship and have fun on the island. But be back here in seven days." The hold empties out in seconds.

A week passes and, of course, the $79-ticket passengers fail to return to the ship. But the cruise line was prepared; they send out squads of big, burly guys who track down the passengers, dragging them kicking and screaming back to the hold. They are again chained to the oars; the drummer takes his position, and "Boom, boom, boom," they row the ship back to New York.

By this time, Kowalski has become good friends with the Armenian. As they are being unchained he says to him, "It is unbelievable that this type of inhuman treatment still exists in the world. This was a living nightmare. But I have to admit it: that guy was a hell of a drummer. Do you think we should tip him?"

The Armenian says, "Well, we didn't last year."

[Admittedly, this is a very contrived joke, but it is a fine one, nonetheless. And, it is a rarity: a joke with three successively funnier punch lines. When you tell the joke, give a little pause between each one.]

My Dad lived to be eighty-six, and in his last years faced several major medical challenges. Though he was often in physical discomfort, he kept his sense of humor. And he did love a good prank. On the evening of December 31, 1999, my Mom, my Dad, and many other members of the First Presbyterian Church in Lebanon (feeling that there was strength in numbers) gathered in the fellowship hall of the church, just in case the Y2K doomsayers were correct and everything went to hell when the New Year arrived. My Dad snuck down to the basement of the church, and, at the stroke of midnight, threw the main circuit breaker, plunging the church into darkness.

He was a funny guy.

Indiana

I was born in Cleveland, Ohio. As I mentioned in the previous chapter, my Dad worked in industry, so we moved around a lot when I was young. We ended up in Fort Wayne, Indiana when I was four. This is when the magic bug bit me. A magician named Dick Stoner did a show at my school. I was probably five years old at the time. I still remember some of the tricks he did. When I was six years old I was given a Sneaky Pete Magic Kit, and I bought tricks from Dick's magic shop. Stoner's funny performing style was a big influence on me.

We moved from Fort Wayne to Lebanon, Indiana in 1963. We made the occasional trek to Fort Wayne so I could buy tricks from Stoner's Magic Shop, and I also ordered things by mail. Dick was (and is) the most exemplary of magic dealers. He never let me buy a trick that was beyond my age or ability.

One time, however, one of Dick's clerks sold me something that wasn't quite appropriate. I wanted to be able to say funny things when I did tricks, so I bought a book of patter lines by Robert Orben. I was probably ten or eleven years old. I read the jokes in the book, and thought they were pretty good. Some of them, however, I didn't really understand. Like an idiot, I told one of *those* jokes to my father:

 Hey Dad, here's my impression of twin beds. [I held both hands out flat, horizontally. I then kept my left hand motionless as my right hand moved up and down.]

I got whacked for that one. Dad also wanted to know where I learned that type of joke. I told him that a kid at school told me, so he wouldn't take away my Orben book. To be honest, I still don't get the joke.

Growing up, I was greatly enamored of performers like Steve Allen, Pete Barbutti, Victor Borge, and Tom Lehrer. I'm sure that one reason that these performers appealed to me so much was that they incorporated the piano into their acts. Lehrer in particular really killed me. His songs were incredibly clever, and his humor was really smart. Several songs (such as *Poisoning Pigeons in the Park*, *The Masochism Tango*, and *I'll Hold Your Hand in Mine*) exemplified a style of humor popular at the time called the "sick" joke. Sometime during my early high school years I bought a small paperback book of sick jokes. I still have that book, but even without referring to it, I can still remember a lot of the jokes.

> Sally: Mrs. Jones, can Billy come out and play baseball?
> Mrs. Jones: Why Sally, you know he has no arms or legs.
> Sally: I know. We want to use him for second base.

*

> A man sees a little boy pushing an iron lung machine down the street. He stops the boy. "Where did you get that iron lung machine?" he asks." "From my father," the boy replies. "Really," says the man. What did your father say?" "Ahhghhhhghhghghhg."
>
> [The "Ahhghhhhghhghghhg" is a long, painful gasp for air.]

*

> What do you call a man with no arms or legs who floats in the ocean? Bob.
>
> What do you call a man with no arms or legs who hangs on a wall? Art.
>
> What do you call a man with no arms or legs who can play seven instruments simultaneously? Stump the Band.

*

A man who is obsessed with sex goes to a psychiatrist. The psychiatrist shows him a rectangle that has been cut from a piece of construction paper. "When you look at this," asks the psychiatrist, "what do you see?" "That's a motel window," says the man, "and there are people screwing behind there."

The psychiatrist shows the man a circle. "How about this?" he asks. "That's a porthole in a cruise ship," the man replies, "and there are people screwing behind there."

"I see," says the psychiatrist. He shows the man a triangle. "What about this?" "That's a keyhole in a bedroom door. There are people screwing behind it."

"Well," says the psychiatrist, "I'm afraid that you are sexually obsessed." "What do you mean *I'm* obsessed?" replies the man. "*You're* the one showing me all the dirty pictures."

And the classic of the genre:

A man and his new bride go to a resort for their honeymoon. The resort offers horseback riding, and the couple decides to give this a try. They have just started off on the trail, when a noise startles the bride's horse. It rears slightly, jostling the bride. The groom jumps off his horse, grabs the reins of the bride's horse, gets right into the horse's face, and says, "That's one."

The couple rides on a bit farther. A small flock of birds, startled by the horses, flies up out of the brush. Again, the bride's horse rears back, and she bounces around on the saddle. The groom jumps off his horse, calms the bride's horse, and says to it, "That's two."

Near the end of the ride, a rabbit runs across the trail. The bride's horse is completely spooked, and the bride is bucked off it. The groom jumps off his horse, makes sure that the bride is unhurt, and then says to the horse, "That's three." He pulls out a gun and shoots the horse in head, killing it.

The bride is appalled. "Oh my god," she says. "You're a sadist. You're a mean-spirited, vicious human being. I can't believe that I married someone as heartless as you." The groom says to her, "That's one."

I grew up in Indiana, and spent most of my adult life there. I like Indiana, and I like the folks who live there. Often, when I perform for a group of people, I begin by talking about my Indiana background.

> I'm originally from Indiana. Are there any Hoosiers in the audience? It's a funny nickname, Hoosiers. I did a show in Sweden a while back, and the Swedes had somehow heard that people from Indiana are called Hoosiers. They asked me, "What does it mean, Hoosiers?" I said that I didn't know; it's just a nickname for people from Indiana. Then they asked me, "On our evening show tonight, would you do something typically Hoosier?" So, I got drunk and didn't show up.

That reminds me...

 A little guy from Valparaiso, Indiana walks into a bar in downtown Chicago. He says to the bartender, "I saw an ad that said you need a bouncer for this bar." The bartender looks at the Hoosier, who is a little, tiny guy. "I don't mean to be rude," he says, "but this is really rough bar; a very tough crowd comes through here."

"Oh, I'm tough," says the little guy. "Really," says the bartender. What's the toughest thing you ever did?"

"Well, back on the farm in Valparaiso, I was driving my Dad's combine when it jammed. When I got off and tried to fix it, it started up all of a sudden, and it ripped my right arm off. I used my belt as a tourniquet on the stump, packed the other part in the ice in my ice chest, drove back to the farmhouse, and sewed it back on by myself."

"Wow," says the bartender. "You are tough! You've got the job."

The little guy says, "All right!" [Hold up both hands in the "thumbs up" position. The right hand, however, is held upside down, with the thumb pointing downward.]

*

A man is using a chainsaw to cut up some wood. The chainsaw hits a knot, springs backward, and cuts off the man's right arm at the elbow. He gets in his car and drives to St. Vincent's hospital. He rushes into the emergency room and explains his predicament to a nurse who is standing by the reception desk. "Come right in," she says. "We'll get you fixed up." "Wait a minute," says the man. "How much is this going to cost me?" "Well, with the surgeon fee, the operating room costs, and the other fees, I would guess about $50,000."

"Forget it," says the man, and he gets in his car and drives to Methodist Hospital. In the emergency room he explains the situation to the receptionist and again asks how much the surgery will cost him. "In the vicinity of $25,000" is the reply. "Forget it," says the man.

He gets back in his car and drives downtown to Wishard Hospital. The only person in the emergency room is a black orderly, who is mopping the floor. The man explains the situation to the orderly. "Well, let's go get you fixed up," says the orderly. "Hang on," says the man. "How much is this going to cost me?" "I don't know for sure, but I'm guessing somewhere around five hundred dollar." "Perfect," says the man, and the orderly takes him back to surgery.

Six weeks later, the man's cast and stitches are removed. Both his arm and his hand work perfectly. He goes back to Saint Vincent's Hospital, walks into the emergency room, and finds the nurse he had originally spoken to.

"Do you remember me?" he asks. "I was in here six weeks ago; my arm had been severed at the elbow. You told me it would cost $50,000 to repair it. I went down to Wishard Hospital, they sewed me back together for $500, and I'm as good as new. All I've got to say to you greedy, scumbag doctors is:" (You hit your left fist against your right elbow joint in the classic "up yours" gesture. Your eyes and head follow your right forearm as it flies over your right shoulder.)

[I have told this joke for many years; it always gets a big laugh. The way I wrote it up is the way I told it when I lived in the Indianapolis area. You will need to adapt it to your locale. Saint Vincent's is the brand new hospital located in the upscale, yuppie section of town. Methodist hospital is located in an older part of Indianapolis, and Wishard is downtown, in an "urban" section of the city. The miming action at the end of the joke is important. You act surprised as your right forearm flies over your shoulder and behind you.]

*

A man is slowly driving down an unpaved country road in Indiana. He glances out the driver-side window and notices that a three-legged chicken is running beside his car. The man speeds up slightly, and the chicken picks up its pace, staying right with the car. The man accelerates again; the chicken matches his speed. The man presses the gas pedal to the floor, racing down the dirt road with the chicken right beside him, pacing his speed.

Just then, the chicken increases its speed, and, like the classic cartoon roadrunner, it zips in front of the car, cuts across the road, heads down a lane, and vanishes from sight. The man brakes, backs up, and turns down the lane, which leads to a farmhouse. A farmer is working in the front yard.

The man gets out of his car. "Did you see a three-legged chicken run past here?" he asks. "Sure did," says the farmer. "Well you're taking it very calmly," says the man. "We raise three-legged chickens on this farm," answers the farmer. "We see them everyday."

"Why in the world would you raise three-legged chickens?" asks the man. "Well, it makes sense," says the farmer. "Let's say you're having chicken for dinner. Maybe you want a drumstick; maybe your wife wants a drumstick; maybe your kid wants a drumstick. You don't need to buy two chickens."

"That's actually a great idea," says the man. "How do they taste?"

"I don't know. We've never been able to catch one."

*

A man is driving down a country road in Indiana when he sees an amazing sight. A farmer is surrounded by several large pigs. He has hoisted one of the pigs up on his shoulders and is allowing the pig to eat his fill of apples from the apple tree he is standing beneath. The man in the car is transfixed; for forty minutes he watches the pig eat apples from the tree. Then, the farmer puts the pig down; he picks up a different pig, and the process starts again. The man can't believe what he's seeing. He gets out of the car and walks over to the farmer.

"What an incredible waste of time," the man says to the farmer.

The farmer replies, "What's time to a pig?"

*

A man is driving down a country road in Indiana. He sees a sign that says, "Pigs for sale – will slaughter." He turns down the lane next to the sign and arrives at a farmhouse. A farmer is standing by a pig pen. "I saw your sign," says the man. "What's the deal with the pigs?"

"It's simple," says the farmer. "You pick out a pig, we'll take it out back, butcher it, and wrap up all the meat for you to take home."

"Okay," says the man, "how much is that pig?" "I don't know," says the farmer, "I'll have to weigh it." The farmer walks into the pen, brings out the designated pig, and pulls the end of the pig's tail so it sticks straight out. The farmer then grabs the pig's tail in his mouth and lifts the pig into air. He holds this position, bent at the waist with the pig hanging from his mouth, for a few seconds and then lets the pig drop to the ground.

"That pig weights forty-six pounds," says the farmer. "Wait a minute," says the man. "This is a scam. You can't weigh a pig like that." "Of course you can," says the farmer. "Everyone around here does it that way. If you want, I'll have my son do it. Hey, Jim, come over here and weigh this pig."

The farmer's son walks over, straightens out the pig's tail, grabs it in his mouth, and lifts it into the air. He holds the pig suspended for a few seconds, and then he drops the pig to the ground. "He weighs forty-six pounds, Dad."

"This is a complete con job," says the man. "Nobody can tell the weight of a pig that way." "You're wrong, stranger," says the farmer. "Everybody does it this way. Jim, run up to the farmhouse and get your mother. Tell her to come out here and weigh this pig."

Jim runs into the farmhouse, is gone for a few moments, and then comes out by himself. "She can't come out right now, Dad," says the son. "It looks like she's about to weigh the milkman."

[I make quite a production out of this joke. To illustrate how the farmer is weighing the pig, I clench my jaw and bend at the waist, holding my hands out to the sides as if maintaining my balance. I love this joke; you just can't see the punch line coming.]

*

A little boy from Valparaiso is batting in his first Little League game. He pops up the ball. It goes over the second baseman's head, but the center fielder had moved up before the pitch. He grabs the ball on the first bounce and whips it to the first baseman. It's close, but the umpire calls the boy out at first. The boy walks back to the dugout and sits down. The coach comes up to him.

"Tell me, Jimmy," says the coach. "When the umpire called you out at first base was it a good thing to yell that he was a blind, fat, son-of-a-bitch?" "No, coach," says Jimmy.

"And when you first came to the ballpark today, was it a good thing to yell at the other team that they were a bunch of pussies?" "No, coach," says Jimmy.

"And when I made you sit out for a couple of innings so little Bobby could get some playing time, was it a good thing to yell at me that I was a stupid bastard who wouldn't know a good player if he bit me in the ass?" "No, coach," says Jimmy.

"In that case, Jimmy, I want you to go up into the stands and tell your grandmother to shut the fuck up."

[You may choose to bowdlerize this punch line, softening it to fit your audience. I have done so myself on occasion, and I'll tell you this: the joke suffers for it. Just remember, Thomas Bowdler was a guy who never got a belly laugh from an audience in his life.]

*

An Indiana farmer is on the witness stand in a trial. He's being questioned by the attorney of the insurance company who represents the young man who ran into the farmer. The farmer had been driving his truck, pulling a trailer, when the young defendant ran into him.

"Here's what I want to know, Mr. Jones," says the attorney. "At the scene of the accident, you told the responding police officer that you were fine. But later, you claimed that you had suffered serious injuries, injuries that you wanted my insurance company to pay for. Why did you change your story?"

"Well, sir," says the farmer, "it was like this. I was driving my truck. I had my best milking cow Bessie in the trailer that I was pulling. That young feller over there ran through a red light and smashed into us. The truck flew over to one side of the road and into a ditch. The trailer landed on the other side of the road and into another ditch.

"I couldn't really move. I heard Bessie bellowing from the other side of the road. Then a police car drove up with its siren blaring. A policeman got out of the car and walked over to the side of the road where Bessie was. He was there for a few moments, and then I heard a gunshot. Then the policeman walked over to me.

"'I'm sorry sir, there was no way to help your cow,' he said to me. 'She was hurt very badly and in a lot of pain, so I put her down...And how are *you* feeling?' What was I *supposed* to say?"

[This is a fine joke. My preferred way of telling it is to leave out the last line ("What was I supposed to say.") and let the joke hang after "So...how are you feeling?" It's much better to let the audience make the necessary connection. I put the last line in just so you know what to say if it looks like nobody is going to get it.]

I don't recall being a class clown in Junior High or High School. Nor did I try to use magic to be the center of attention. (Although as a fat, smart, insecure kid I certainly could have used all the help I could get.) I was more content laughing at other people's jokes. One of the people who made me laugh was a kid named Bill Dazey, who was one of my best friends at the time. In many of our classes the students were seated alphabetically, which meant that Bill was often seated behind me. I remember an incident in Sophomore English; we were studying Sophocles' immortal tragedy *Oedipus Rex*. The teacher said, "Let's begin our discussion by answering a basic question: What do the words *Oedipus Rex* mean?" I made eye contact with the teacher. Bill leaned forward and whispered, "Mother fucker." Well, this killed me. I tried to keep a straight face, but I failed miserably. I put my head down on my desk and laughed uncontrollably.

My memory is a little hazy, but I think Bill Dazey told me this joke:

> A collegiate heavyweight wrestler from the University of Illinois makes it to the final round of the NCAA wrestling championship. His opponent in the final round is a wrestler from Texas State University. The Texan has a secret weapon, a submission hold called the "Pretzel Hold." The Texan has won each of his tournament matches with a pin, and each pin was the direct result of the pretzel hold. Once the pretzel hold was in place, his opponents were unable to move; as they fought the hold they weakened themselves, and they were eventually pinned.
>
> The afternoon before the final match, the U of I coach meets with his wrestler. "Listen," he tells him, "I've been up all night watching films of that Texas wrestler.

I can't figure out any way to reverse the pretzel hold. So here's what I want you to do. I want you to keep away from him; try to put your own moves on him – you're a really great wrestler. But if he gets you in the pretzel hold, I want you to give up. I don't want you to be seriously injured just for the sake of a trophy. It's not worth it."

The match starts. Both wrestlers are excellent athletes, and at the end of the first two rounds the score is tied. The third round starts with the U of I wrestler in the "down" position. The referee blows his whistle, and the Texas wrestler immediately puts on the pretzel hold. A long moan escapes from the Illinois fans. Both wrestlers are motionless for thirty seconds. Just then, the Illinois wrestler moves with unbelievable speed. He performs an amazing reversal, spins the Texas wrestler onto his back, and pins him.

The crowd goes wild. The Illinois fans lift their wrestler up on their shoulders and carry him around the gymnasium. It's a full twenty minutes before the coach is able to take the wrestler aside and talk to him. "How did you do it?" he asks. "I couldn't find any way to break that hold."

"Well, coach," says the wrestler, "it was really tough. He's a great wrestler. I tried to keep away from him and put on my own holds, just like you said. But at the start of the third round I couldn't get away, and he put the pretzel hold on me. It was terrible. I couldn't move; I couldn't breathe. I was just about to give up, when I glanced over my right shoulder. I could see a pair of balls hanging right there. I was desperate coach, so I bit them as hard as I could. And coach, you wouldn't believe how fast you can move when you bite your own balls."

I graduated from Lebanon High School in 1970. In 1990, I served as the Master of Ceremonies at my twenty-year class reunion. I wrote a pretty good joke for that occasion. The attendees received a booklet that had each of our senior pictures, plus information about what we now did for a living, spouses, children, etc. Here's the joke.

I have to confess that looking through the souvenir booklet made me feel a little old. Especially when I realized that the girl I dated in high school now has a daughter who's older than I was when her mother dumped me.

From 1988 to 1998 I lived in Carmel, Indiana, a northern suburb of Indianapolis. Carmel was yuppie central, an affluent, upscale community. For five years I worked at a magic-themed restaurant called Illusions, which was located in Carmel. There was a small stage in the bar, suitable for stand-up magic shows. During my shows I always told a lot of Carmel jokes.

> I met a Carmel hooker last night on my way home. I didn't even know that such a thing existed. I said to her, "What's the deal?" She said, "You give me $500 and I'll do anything you want." So, she got in the car and we drove back to my place.
>
> We got out of the car and I gave her the $500. "What are we going to do?" she asked. "I'm going to bed," I replied. "You're going to paint the house."

*

> A Carmel yuppie is talking to his wife. "I would find it very arousing if you would moan when we make love. Could you do that for me?" "Sure," says the wife.
>
> So, that night, the yuppie snuggles with his wife. He plays with her hair and lightly runs his fingers along her arms. "Now?" the wife asks. "Do you want me to moan now?" "No, not yet," says the yuppie.
>
> They crawl under the covers. The yuppie kisses the back of his wife's neck and gently fondles her breasts. "Now?" the wife asks. "Do you want me to moan now?" "No, not now," says the yuppie.
>
> Finally, they begin to make love. "Now?" the wife asks. "Do you want me to moan now?" "Yes!" says the yuppie. "Moan now."
>
> "Ooooooh," the wife says. "What a day I had today. First I had to take the kids to school, and then I had to buy groceries…"

*

I was driving around Carmel yesterday, and I came to an intersection where the cross traffic had the right of way. Traffic was pretty heavy, but I saw an opportunity, a break in the traffic. Instead of coming to a full stop, I slowed down and made a right-hand turn. I had no sooner made the turn, when a Carmel cop put on his flashers and pulled me over.

"You didn't stop at that intersection," he said to me. "I know officer," I replied. "But I did slow down and check for oncoming traffic."

"Yes, but you didn't stop." "No, I didn't. But I did slow down."

"But you didn't stop." "No," I said, "I didn't stop, but I did slow down. What the hell is the difference?"

The cop took out his nightstick and started to hit me with it. "Now, what do you want me to do," he asked, "slow down or stop?"

The previous joke was a favorite of Terry Veckey, a clever Chicago magician who moved to Indianapolis to be part of the Illusions staff. I'm reminded that Terry often told this joke:

- A man runs into a former high school classmate, who, surprisingly, looks like a pirate. Not only is he dressed like a pirate, he has a hook on his right hand, a peg leg, an eye patch, and a parrot on his shoulder. "Jim, is that you?" asks the man. "You look like a pirate." "I am a pirate," says Jim. "I joined a pirate crew right after I left high school."

  "How did you lose your leg?" asks the man. "It was when we boarded an enemy ship," Jim answers. "It was my first sword fight. I made an awkward move and the guy I was fighting cut off my leg. I replaced it with a peg leg."

  "What happened to your hand?" asks the man. "Ah, that happened during my second sword fight. I wasn't used to the peg leg. I lost my balance, and the guy I was fighting cut off my hand. I replaced it with a hook."

- "Well, what happened to your eye?" "That happened one afternoon when I was in the crow's nest. I was looking up, and a seagull crapped in my eye."

"Seagull poop makes you lose your eye?" asks the man. Jim replies, "It does when you forget your hand is a hook."

*

- We had some excitement here at Illusions last night. One of our Carmel yuppies lost control of his car and smashed into a tree just outside the restaurant. We all heard the noise and ran out to help. This fellow had not been wearing his seatbelt, and he was thrown from the car. In the process, his left arm had been torn off. When we got to him he was walking around his smashed car muttering, "My Porsche, my Porsche!"

I said to him, "Hey pal, you have a bigger problem than that. You've lost your arm."

He said, "My Rolex, my Rolex!"

[When I mention that the yuppie has lost his arm, I always stick my left hand into my jacket (or pants) pocket to provide visual reinforcement. I'm fond of this joke. Telling it provides a way to accomplish some sneaky magical stuff.]

*

- A postman has been delivering mail in Carmel for many years. He is finally retiring, and is making his rounds for the last time. When he gets to the Jones house, Mrs. Jones opens the front door. She is wearing a very slinky negligee. "This is your last day, isn't it?" she asks. "Yes it is," says the mailman. "Would you like to come inside and have some breakfast?" "Why yes, that would be nice."

The mailman follows Mrs. Jones into the house. He sits at the kitchen table and she serves him a sumptuous breakfast of fresh fruit, crispy bacon, and Belgian waffles. When he finishes eating, Mrs. Jones grabs his hand and leads him upstairs to the bedroom, where they proceed to make passionate love. As they are putting their clothes back on, Mrs. Jones reaches into her purse and hands the mailman a five-dollar bill.

"I'm sorry," says the postman. "I don't understand. What's going on here?"

"Well," says Mrs. Jones, "last night I mentioned to my husband that you were retiring, and that today was going to be your last day. I asked him what we should do for you. He said, 'Screw him. Give him five dollars.' Breakfast was my idea."

*

A Carmel yuppie has spent Saturday night drinking with his buddies; he comes home at two in the morning roaring drunk. He unlocks the front door, and just as he opens it, he throws up. The dog, hearing the noise, runs to the foyer, and the man throws up all over the dog. He then slips in the vomit, falls on the dog, and they both roll around in the muck. The man's wife comes downstairs, and as she tries to help her husband up the stairs he throws up on her, the dog, and the stairs. She finally gets him to the bedroom, where he promptly passes out.

The next morning, he awakes and finds himself completely cleaned up, lying in satin sheets. Next to the bed is a tray with a glass of freshly-squeezed orange juice, two aspirin, and a note. The note reads, "I've gone to the store for beer and munchies. I know how much you enjoy them when you're watching the Sunday football games. Your breakfast is in the refrigerator; just pop it in the microwave. I'll be home soon."

The man staggers downstairs, unable to comprehend what has gone on. His teenaged son is in the kitchen, reading the newspaper. "Do you have any idea what happened last night?" the man asks.

"From what I understand, Dad, you came home really drunk last night. You threw up on the front stoop, you threw up on the dog, you threw up on Mom, and you threw up on the stairs. Mom got you into the bedroom, and as she was trying to get you undressed you said to her, 'Get your hands off me, bitch; I'm married!'"

[How lovely – a fidelity joke.]

Let's wrap up this chapter with two more Indiana farmer jokes.

> An Indiana chicken farmer needs a new rooster. He's owned his current rooster for a long time, and the old bird just can't perform his necessary duties. The farmer buys a new, young rooster and puts him out in the barnyard.
>
> The old rooster walks up to the young one. "Listen," he says, "I know why you're here. I'm getting old, and there's no way I can do my job the way I used to. Once you start performing, there'll be no reason to keep me around. They'll take me in the back, cut off my head, and make soup out of me.
>
> "I don't want to go out that way, so I want you to do me a favor. Fight me. You're younger and stronger, and I know that you'll kill me, but at least I'll go out fighting."
>
> The young rooster says, "That's an amazing attitude to take; you're one hell of a rooster. I'm honored to have known you, if only for a short time. I promise that when the end comes, I'll make it quick and painless. Let's fight."
>
> The young rooster lunges for the older one, but instead of attacking, the old rooster runs away. The young rooster is dumbfounded, and he starts to chase the old rooster around the barnyard. Just then, the farmer appears on his front porch with a rifle in hand. He takes aim and blows the young rooster away. He yells to his wife, "Dammit, Bertha, that's the fourth queer rooster I've bought this week."

*

- A man is driving down a country road in Indiana. He passes a farm house, and in the front yard he sees a three-legged pig. His curiosity gets the best of him, so he stops, backs up, and drives down the lane to the farmhouse. A farmer comes out of the garage.

    "Excuse me," says the man, "but did I see a three-legged pig?" "That's right," says the farmer. The man's curiosity is piqued. He asks, "Why does the pig have only three legs?"

"Well, that's an interesting story," the farmer says. "When that pig was just a piglet he heard a fox that had gotten into the hen house. The piglet chased the fox away and saved all the hens. A year later I was plowing my field and my tractor flipped over, trapping me underneath. I yelled, and the pig heard me. He ran out to the field and dug a little trough so I could crawl out. And then last year one of our lamps short circuited. The house caught on fire. The pig smelled the smoke, ran into the house and dragged my wife and me to safety."

"That's all very interesting," says the man, "but why does the pig have only three legs?"

"Gosh mister, a special pig like that you can't eat all at once."

Michael B.

After high school, I attended Purdue University and attempted to be a mathematics major. I was good at math and science, but after two years I realized that my heart wasn't in it, and I transferred to the music school at Butler University (in Indianapolis) as a Music Theory and Composition major. During my last year at Purdue I had discovered some music theory texts in the main library, and I studied them well enough to earn credit for freshman music theory at Butler.

My first class at Butler was sophomore music theory. I had the embarrassing job of standing in front of a group of people I didn't know and announcing that the professor was going to be a few minutes late. (I had run into him on my way into the building, and he asked that I make the announcement.) I sat down next to a tall guy with dark brown hair and a thick beard. He welcomed me to the class. (Actually, I think he said, "Who the hell are you?") His name was Michael Bryant, and it took all of about two minutes for us to realize that we were brothers from separate mothers. We hit it off immediately. We were in many of the same classes, and we sang together in the Contemporary Choir. It was on a road trip with this choir that Michael told me the greatest joke I have ever heard at 2 a.m. while riding a bus. The choir had performed in Chicago, and the bus driver got lost trying to get out of town, so what should have been a four-hour bus ride became an all-night tour of the back roads of northwestern Indiana. Several of us had been telling jokes to pass the time, and Michael dropped this bomb on us.

- Two gentlemen are sitting in the library of the British Explorers Club. They have just had a marvelous meal, and they are enjoying cigars and brandy. One says to the other, "I say, Chauncey, have I ever told you the story of my hunt for the king of beasts, the mighty lion?"

"Why no, Edgar, I don't think you have recounted that particular adventure," says his friend.

"Ah, dreadfully exciting it was. There we were in Tanzania, in the heart of the Serengeti, crawling on our bellies through the high elephant grass. My faithful guide Umgubu was behind me. We reached the edge of the grass, and there, in a clearing under an umbrella tree, munching on the carcass of a zebra was the great beast himself – the mighty lion.

"I stood, and Umgubu handed me my rifle. I took careful aim and fired. Click! A misfire. I rapidly ejected that shell and loaded another. I drew a bead and...Click! Another misfire. By this time, the beast had picked up our scent. He rose, he turned, he charged...ROAR! Well, by jove, I shit my pants."

"Well, Edgar, that's nothing to be ashamed of. The beast had the bloodlust, your weapon failed to respond, a horrible death was imminent. In that situation anyone would have done the same."

"No, no, not then. Just now, when I went, 'ROAR!'"

[There will be a strong tendency for the audience to laugh at the shock line ("I shit my pants") and you will need to shut down that laugh. I do this by charging straight into the next line ("Well, Edgar"). This is another joke that I pour my heart into, doing the voices, standing up and gesturing wildly when I say "Roar." It's a wonderful joke.]

Michael Bryant and I worked together often after college; we played together in bands, and we had a music production company. We wrote jingles, composed and produced music for industrial videos, and even wrote the score for an absolutely horrible movie called *Good Cop, Bad Cop*. (You have heard of movies that go straight to video; this movie went straight to dumpster. And the dumpster was in Korea.) I've made a lot of music with a lot of different people in my life, but the times I spent working with Michael were the best times of my life. As we worked we laughed and laughed.

At Butler I also met John Hill, a very fine percussionist who now teaches at Murray State University in Kentucky. John and I worked together a great deal; he was the drummer in the first jazz trio I led. The very first time John and I played a paying gig together was at a wedding reception. John had booked the gig; I didn't know any of the people involved. The reception was held in the fellowship hall of a church. The band was set up in a corner of the room. The plan was that when the ceremony was finished, the attendees would file into the hall for food. We were told to start the music when the bride and groom entered. People filtered in, and then someone announced, "Here they come." I turned to John and the bass player and said, "*Night and Day*." I counted off, and we launched into the well-known Cole Porter tune. The bride and groom walked into the fellowship hall. She was black; he was white. It's a good thing no one ever listens to the background music. (Although sometimes they do, as you will read at the end of this chapter.)

I had more fun my first week at Butler than I did in two years at Purdue. Musicians have a particular sensibility (without which they probably wouldn't be musicians) that I share. Because of their outlook on life, musicians are rich fodder for jokes, and I have told a lot of musician jokes. There are, of course, the simple insult jokes:

> Q: What do you call a drummer without a girlfriend?
> A: Homeless.
>
> Q: What do you say to a drummer in a three-piece suit?
> A: "Will the defendant please rise."
>
> Q: What does a drummer get on his IQ test?
> A: Saliva.
>
> Q: What does it mean if drool is coming out of both sides of a drummer's mouth?
> A: The stage is perfectly level.
>
> Q: What has three legs and a dick?
> A: A drum stool.
>
> Q: What is perfect pitch?
> A: Being able to throw a clarinet into a toilet without hitting the rim.

Q: A snake and a conductor are lying dead in the road. What's the difference between them?
A: There are skid marks in front of the snake.

Q: What's the difference between a violin and a viola?
A: The viola burns longer.

Q: What's the difference between an accordion and an onion?
A: Nobody cries when you chop up an accordion.

Q: What's the difference between a jazz musician and a large pizza?
A: The pizza can feed a family of four.

Q: What do trombone players use for birth control?
A: Their personalities.

Q: How many country western singers does it take to screw in a light bulb?
A: Five. One to screw in the bulb, and the other four to sing about how much they miss the old light bulb.

Q: How many music producers does it take to screw in a light bulb?
A: Geez, I don't know. What do you think?

[The great thing about the above jokes is that they are adaptable. Many of them work with "magician" as the subject.]

And that reminds me:

> The scene is a cavalry fort in the middle of Indian territory. The time is that moment in the early morning just before the sun comes over the horizon. In a turret in the fort, a cavalry colonel, his steel-gray hair neatly combed, stands looking out at the plains. There is just enough light to make out vague shapes; the colonel can see that the fort is surrounded by Indians. They are about 100 yards from the fort, and their numbers continue as far as the eye can see.
>
> Just then, the sun peeks over the horizon, and the soldiers can hear the sound of the Indian drums, "Boom, boom, boom, boom. Boom, boom, boom, boom." The

colonel turns to his sergeant. "I don't like the sound of those drums," he says.

From the mass of Indians a voice calls out, "He's not our regular drummer!"

*

An American is exploring the jungles of Africa for the first time. He and his guide reach a small clearing just as the sun is beginning to set. All of a sudden, the sounds of drums can be heard, "Boom, boom, boom, boom. Boom, boom, boom, boom." The American is a little spooked. "What's up with the drums?" he asks his guide. "It's nothing," the guide replies. "At this time of day the natives like to unwind a little. It's nothing to worry about. There would only be a problem if the drums stopped."

The two men set up camp, building a small fire to cook food. As they eat, the drums continue, "Boom, boom, boom, boom. Boom, boom, boom, boom." "I'm really freaked out about those drums," says the American. "Relax, relax," says the guide. "There's no problem unless the drums stop."

The American and the guide crawl into their sleeping bags. The campfire dies, and, just as the last ember goes out, the men hear, "Boom, boom, boom, boom. Boom, boom, boom, boom. Boom…" And then silence. "Uh oh," says the guide. "What happens now?" asks the American. The guide replies, "Bass solo."

*

On the afternoon of December 31st, a club owner gets a call from the leader of the band he has hired for his New Year's Eve party. There has been a death in the family, and since all the members of the band are related, none will be able to make the gig. The club owner is without entertainment on the biggest party night of the year.

He calls every agent and booker in town trying to find a band. The only musicians available are a duo – an accordion player and a tuba player. The club owner is skeptical, but he's also desperate, so he hires the duo.

The duo starts to play at 9 p.m. that night. Immediately the dance floor is filled with happy partiers. For four hours people are dancing, laughing, and having fun. The party is a tremendous success.

At 1 a.m. the club owner comes up to the duo as they're packing up their instruments. "I have to confess," he says. "I really didn't think this was going to work out, but you guys were terrific. All I heard were compliments; everyone had a wonderful time. You really pulled my fat out of the fire, and right now I want to hire you for next year. Will you do it?"

"Sure," says the accordion player. "Is it okay if we leave our stuff?"

*

A visitor to New York City goes to a jazz club to hear a famous saxophone player. The visitor is a big fan, and he can hardly wait to hear the jazzer play live.

The saxophonist walks into the club, heads straight to the bar, orders two double scotches, and immediately tosses both of them straight back. He orders two more drinks, and carries them up to the bandstand. He drinks both of them as he unpacks his sax. Then he heads back to the bar, and while the other members of the band arrive and set up, he downs three more double scotches.

The jazzer carries two more drinks up on stage. Before the set is over, the cocktail waitress has brought him two more. The music, however, is incredible; the saxophonist is a monster. His playing burns up the stage.

The sax player steps off the stage, heads back to the bar, and orders another drink. The visitor has been overwhelmed by the music. Stunned and awed, he approaches the sax player. "That was some of the greatest music I've ever heard," he says. "How in the world can you drink so much and play so well?" "Oh, it's simple," says the sax player. "I practice drunk."

*

A jazz musician goes to the doctor. The doctor says, "We have your test results, and I'm afraid the news isn't good. You have three weeks to live." The jazzer says, "On what?"

*

A little boy comes home from school dragging an acoustic bass behind him. As he enters the living room his father says, "Hey, what's with the bass?" The little boy says, "The conductor of the middle school orchestra came to home room today and gave us an aptitude test. My test showed that I should play the bass, so tomorrow I start orchestra class." "That's great," says the father, "keep me updated."

The next day, the boy walks into his house, dragging the bass behind him. "How was orchestra?" asks the father. "Orchestra was great. Today we learned all about the E string. At the end of the class we played rhythms on the E string." "Wonderful," says the father.

The next day, the father asks the same question, "How was orchestra, son?" "It was great, Dad. We learned about the A string. We played rhythms on the A string, and then at the end of class we played rhythms back and forth between the A string and the E string."

The next day, the boy walks into the living room dragging his bass behind him. "How was orchestra, son?" the father asks. "I didn't go, Dad. I had a gig."

[This is another musician joke that, with some minor adjustments, works well as a magician joke.]

*

A rock band has just signed a deal with a big record label. There will be a major press conference/media event the next day announcing the contract and the upcoming worldwide concert tour. The record company will be throwing their entire P.R. department behind the band, guaranteeing that today is their last day of anonymity.

However, that evening the band has one more gig to fulfill at a small venue in their home town. As they launch into their opening song, the lead guitar player thinks to himself, "This is the last crummy gig I ever play. After tomorrow it's going to be great venues, private jets, five-star hotels, roadies at my beck and call, and every perk I can ask for."

The rhythm guitar player thinks to himself, "After tomorrow I'm going to party like no one has ever partied before. It's going to be non-stop drinking, designer drugs, and top-shelf women."

The drummer thinks to himself, "Tomorrow starts the next big step for me. In two years I'm going to ditch these losers and launch a solo career, with my band, playing my music."

The bass player thinks to himself, "A, A, A, A, E, E, A, A, G, G, A, A..."

*

A man is walking on 57th Street, near Carnegie Hall. He passes a pawn shop. In the window of the shop is a beautiful violin. The man has listened to music all his life, but has never played an instrument, and yet the violin seems to be calling out to him. He walks into the pawn shop and asks the clerk if he can play the violin. The clerk says, sure. The man takes the violin from the window, rosins the bow, and begins to play the Largo movement from Bach's *Double Concerto*. Although this man has never touched a violin before, the music he produces is exquisite. The clerk is moved to tears.

The manager of Carnegie Hall happens to be walking by the pawn shop and hears the music. The beauty of it stops him in his tracks. He walks into the shop. "That is the most wonderful violin playing I have ever heard," he tells the man. "Will you play a concert at Carnegie Hall?" "What the hell, why not?" says the man.

The man performs at Carnegie Hall. Attending the concert are music critics from around the world and the elite of New York society. The music is sublime, but there is something else. As the man plays, a feeling of serenity embraces the audience; all the anger and frustration they feel fade away. The audience leaves the concert hall filled with happiness and love.

One of the attendees is the Secretary General of the United Nations. He goes backstage after the concert and says to the man, "Your playing has the ability to instill peace and tranquility. We want you to travel under the auspices of the U.N. and play concerts in the trouble-spots of the world. Will you do it?" "Sure, why the hell not?" says the man.

So, the man travels around the world. He plays in Iraq, and the sectarian violence ends. He plays in the Gaza Strip, and the troubles between the Israelis and the Palestinians ends. He travels to Rwanda, and the ethnic cleansing stops.

The evening after his Rwandan concert, the man hears a knock on the window of his ground-floor hotel room. He opens his window, and is surprised to be face to face with a lioness. "I'm sorry to bother you," says the lioness. "The animals of the jungle have heard about your amazing abilities on the violin. The jungle is an extremely violent place; we were hoping that you would come into the jungle and play for us. Will you?" "Sure," says the man, "why the hell not?"

The man follows the lioness into the jungle. They walk for an hour, eventually reaching a clearing in the heart of the jungle. The man takes out his violin and begins to play Vaughn Williams' *A Lark Ascending*. The music rises and spreads through the treetops. Suddenly, animals appear. The lion lies down with the lamb; the cobra snuggles up to the mongoose. The clearing fills with animals of all types, in utter serenity, transfixed by the music.

Suddenly, a tiger leaps into the clearing. He jumps on the man. He eats the violin; he eats the man; he eats the man's clothes; he eats the violin case. There is nothing left. The lioness is appalled. She screams at the tiger, "How could you do this? He was making such beautiful music! Everyone was calm; everyone was peaceful. What's wrong with you?"

And the tiger says, [putting his paw to his ear] "Eh!?"

[Okay, okay. I admit that this is a shaggy dog joke. You may want to edit it down to its bare bones when you tell it, but I like the verisimilitude that the details add. Be sure to cup your hand to your ear when you say, "Eh." With a joke this long, you want the punch line to be clear.]

*

Jascha Heifetz is touring the United States, bringing his music to as many people as possible. His tour takes him out west, and very early one morning he arrives in Helena, Montana. He checks into his hotel just as a light snow begins to fall. The snowstorm becomes a blizzard, dumping several feet of snow on the city. Heifetz walks across the street to the concert hall. Peeking through the curtain, he sees that only six people are in the theatre. He steps through the curtain and addresses the small audience.

"My friends," he says, "my thanks for coming out in such inclement weather. There being so few of you, perhaps our time together would be better served by walking across the street to my hotel. There is a fine restaurant there with a warm, inviting fireplace. I would be happy to buy dinner for all of you, and we can spend the evening with food, drink, and conversation."

A man in the audience stands up. "Excuse me, Mr. Heifetz. I've been waiting for this concert for months. I had to schedule three extra days of work so the ranch boss would let me off today. I spent four hours walking through snow that was up to my neck just to get here. So, if it's all the same to you, just shut up and sing."

*

As part of his tour, Heifetz finds himself in a small town in Kansas. The people are nice, but unsophisticated. The program Heifetz has chosen for the tour includes Bach's D minor Chaconne, from the *Second Partita* for solo violin. Feeling that the Chaconne will be beyond the taste of the locals, Heifetz substitutes a more accessible piece, a flashy theme and variations on a folk tune.

After the concert, Heifetz stands in the lobby, signing autographs. A man comes up to him. "Mr. Heifetz, sir," the man says, "I've been reading about your tour. You didn't play the Bach Chaconne tonight." Heifetz is dumbfounded. "My dear sir," he says. "I had no idea that anyone in this town would care one way or the other. Please come to my hotel. We will have dinner, and then I will give you a private performance of the Chaconne."

The men return to Heifetz' hotel, have an excellent dinner, and retire to Heifetz' suite. Heifetz tunes up and launches into the monumentally difficult Chaconne, finishing thirteen minutes later. He looks at his sole audience member.

"So," says the man, "that's the Chaconne. First time I've heard it. I don't care for it."

*

The mass has begun at a Catholic Church. A few minutes into the proceedings the priest steps away from the pulpit. He faces the congregation and chants, "I am the priest of this church. I make four hundred dollars a month, and that's not enough to live on."

A little later in the service the assistant to the priest steps forward and chants, "I am the assistant to the priest of this church. I make two hundred dollars a month, and that's not enough to live on."

A few minutes pass. The assistant to the assistant to the priest steps forward and chants, "I am the assistant to the assistant to the priest of this church. I make one hundred dollars a month, and that's not enough to live on."

Near the end of the service, the organist sticks his head out of the organ loft and chants, "I am the organist of this church. I make eight hundred dollars a *week*, and there's no business like show business, like no business I know..."

[This joke may not read well, but it explodes in the telling. The last line is sung to the classic *There's No Business Like Show Business* song. This is a great joke

>   for the stage, especially if you are working with a live musician who can play along with the final line. I have performed it this way several times with my friend, the very funny Rich Bloch.]

One year, during the Christmas season, John Hill called me with a desperate request. A drum student of his had accepted a Christmas party gig without checking to see if he could find the necessary players. He was short a piano player and was in a panic. "Is there any chance you could play this gig?" John asked. Well, as it turned out, I had not booked any gigs on that particular Saturday, because I was planning to attend the Indianapolis Symphony Orchestra Christmas concert. John had helped me out of plenty of jams, so I was happy to return the favor. I told him I would play the gig with his student.

When I got to the gig I discovered that we were playing a Korean Christmas party. It looked as if every Korean in Indianapolis was in attendance. They had a Korean emcee, and Korean decorations adorned the hall. I set up my gear and introduced myself to the 19-year-old drummer. He was freaked out. "What in the world are we going to play?" he asked me. I replied, "Anything but the *Theme from M.A.S.H.*"

The following jokes are more esoteric. They are funnier if you know a bit about music. Tell them to a group of musicians and you'll get roars.

> A drummer gets a gig in Turkey. Unfortunately, he knows nothing about Turkish music. He gets to Ankara, hauls his gear to the gig, and begins to set up his drums. The band leader arrives, and the drummer introduces himself, confessing that he knows nothing about Turkish music. "Is okay," says the leader. "Music is very simple. Just needs heavy backbeat on 2 and 13."

>   *

> The Indianapolis Symphony Orchestra is on a three-week tour of Europe. Their first performance is in Paris. After the concert the members of the orchestra head out to enjoy the fine dining Paris offers. Unfor-

tunately, the conductor eats some tainted escargot, and he comes down with food poisoning. He is out of commission for seven days, during which time the concertmaster conducts the orchestra. On the eighth day, the conductor is well enough to continue his duties, at a concert in Hamburg. As he walks toward the podium, the assistant concertmaster turns to the concertmaster and says, "Where the hell have you been for the past week?"

*

A couple have been married for many years, and during that time they have become less and less communicative. It has reached the point where they simply refuse to talk to each other. The situation is driving their children nuts, so they arrange for the couple to meet with a therapist. For three months the therapist tries to break the couple's verbal impasse, but to no avail. One day, when the couple arrive for their session, they are greeted with grim news.

"I've worked with you for three months now," says the therapist, "trying to get you two to communicate. Nothing has worked. I have one more thing to try, but if this doesn't work, you are going to have to find another doctor." So saying, the therapist walks to a closet and brings out an acoustic bass. The therapist begins to play an improvised jazz solo on the bass, and the couple start talking to each other.

*

A jazz saxophonist dies. He awakes and discovers that he is sitting in the saxophone section of a big band. He looks around; Lester Young and Coleman Hawkins are sitting next to him. "This is heaven," says the sax player. "No," says the Hawk, "this is hell. Just wait until Bones gets here." Duke Ellington walks in and sits down at the piano. Charles Mingus walks in with a bass. "This must be heaven," says the jazzer. "No," says Hawkins, "it's hell. Just wait until Bones gets here." Maynard Ferguson, Louis Armstrong, and Bix Beiderbecke sit down in the trumpet section. "This has to be heaven," says the jazzer. "No, it's hell," says the Hawk. "Here comes Bones."

Karen Carpenter walks in, sits down at the drums, and says, "Okay, here we go: *Close to You*. One, two, one, two, three, four..."

*

A crowd has gathered on a street in New York. A man is standing on a ledge, ten stories up, and he is threatening to jump. Someone in the crowd yells up to him, "Don't jump, man. Why do you want to jump?"

The man on the ledge says, "I'm a jazz saxophone player. No one wants to hear my music. No one appreciates me. No one understands what I'm trying to do. I'm going to jump."

The guy on the ground says, "You can't jump, man. You can't give up. Bird never gave up."

The guy on the ledge says, "Who's Bird?"

The guy on the ground says, "Jump, motherfucker."

I'm not a big fan of singers. I have worked with a few who are good, competent musicians, but far too often I have found that singers are pampered, coddled, babies whose mistakes have to be covered up by the musicians who accompany them.

> Q: How many chick singers does it take to screw in a light bulb?
> A: One, but she just stands still and lets the world revolve around her.

When I moved to Las Vegas I was scrambling to find work. A friend of mine knew a piano player whose girlfriend was looking for an accompanist. (To keep the relationship peaceful, the piano player chose not to work with his girlfriend. Smart move.) My friend gave me the singer's phone number. I called and explained that if the singer was going to perform standard tunes, she should simply fax me a list of fifty songs she would like to sing and the keys she does those tunes in. I would learn the tunes in her keys, and, since I had been accompanying singers since I was seventeen, we wouldn't even need a rehearsal. I would make it sound as if we had been working together for years.

The singer faxed me the list on a Monday. She didn't do any of the songs in the keys that I was familiar with, but that was okay; it's good practice to learn tunes in different keys. I worked on the songs for a week, and we met up at the club on Friday night.

The club had a nice grand piano, which was a bonus. I asked the singer what song she'd like to start with, and she suggested *Bye Bye Blackbird*, a fine choice. She counted off the tune, I played an intro, she sang through the tune, I played a solo chorus, she sang through it a final time, and we did a big tag. It was perfect, and the crowd appreciated it.

She acknowledged the applause, and introduced herself and me. And the very next words out of her mouth (and I swear that this is true) were, "Does anybody have any requests?"

I had no choice but to hold up my hand. "Yeah, I got a request. How about we stick to the goddamn list."

> A female singer and her accompanist are about to begin a set. "Let's start with *On a Clear Day*," she suggests. "Okay," says the pianist. "When you do it tonight, leave out the fifth bar, go up a whole step at the start of the second verse, go to the bridge two bars early, and jump back to the original key four bars before the end."
>
> "I don't think I can sing it that way," says the singer.
>
> "Really? That's the way you sang it last night."

*

> A female singer is working with an accompanist she hasn't worked with before. The gig is going well until someone in the audience yells out a request for *Misty*. She turns to the piano player and says, "It's been a long time since I've sung that. I'm not sure I can remember it all." The piano player says, "Don't worry, I'll help you out."

> The pianist plays an intro, the singer sings, "Look at me…" and goes completely blank. She looks at the piano player, who whispers to her, "B flat minor 7th."

Playing cocktail piano can be a tough gig. There is no getting around the fact that you are providing ambient background noise, and few people are actually listening to what you are playing. The hardest part of a cocktail piano gig is the moment when you finish a song and you have to decide what song to play next. The silence that accompanies this thought process is a grim reminder that you are really just playing to the walls. To circumvent this problem I use an idea I learned from listening to the great jazz pianist Dave McKenna – I organize tunes into long medleys. I string together fourteen or fifteen songs into a forty-five-minute medley (analogous to the way I remember jokes). In this way, I never worry about what song is coming next, and the evening flies by quickly.

Some years ago I was playing solo piano at the Restaurant in the Eiffel Tower at the Paris Resort and Casino in Las Vegas. I was in the middle of a long George Gershwin medley. A man walked up to the piano with a five-dollar bill in his hand. He said to me, "Could you play some Gershwin songs?" I shifted from the tune I was playing into a vamp, and said to him, "I've been playing Gershwin tunes for the past twenty minutes, and I'll be playing Gershwin tunes for twenty-five minutes more. I'm in the middle of a big Gershwin medley." He looked at me and said (and I'm not making this up), "Do I still need to tip you?"

> A man is playing cocktail piano in the lounge of a country club. A Japanese man walks up to him and says, "Play jazz chord!" The pianist stops the song he was playing and launches into George Gershwin's *Our Love is Here to Stay*, sprucing up the tune with plenty of interesting harmonic substitutions.
>
> The Japanese man walks back to the piano and interrupts the pianist saying, "No, no. Play jazz chord!" The pianist begins to play Thelonius Monk's *Well You Needn't*, adorning the song with plenty of dissonant minor seconds and "outside" chord changes.
>
> "No, no, no!" says the Japanese man. "Play jazz chord!"

"Listen," says the pianist, "I have no idea what you want. Why don't you play it."

The Japanese man sits down at the piano, plays a short introduction, and sings, "Jazz chord to say, I love you…"

[Of course, the last line is sung to the tune of Stevie Wonder's *Just Called to Say I Love You*.]

*

A fellow is singing and playing cocktail piano at a club in New York. A big guy walks up to the piano. He's about six foot four, and from the look of his nose, he's been in a few fights. He says to the piano player, "Do you take requests?" The piano player says, "If I know the song, I'd be happy to do it for you."

"Okay," says the big man, "here's what I wants you to do. Youse should play *Strangers in the Night*, key of D flat, 5/4 time." "The key of D flat is no problem," says the piano player, "but *Strangers in the Night* is normally in 4/4 time, not 5/4 time."

"I didn't asks you to tell me about normals," replies the big man. "Youse should play *Strangers in the Night*, key of D flat, 5/4 time. I'm gonna sing." "Well," says the piano player, "I'm not exactly sure what the establishment's policy is about letting patrons sing…"

Just then, the guy's coat opens a bit and the piano player can see a big gun hanging from a shoulder holster. He immediately launches into a weird 5/4 introduction in the key of D flat.

The big guy picks up the microphone and sings, "Strangers in the fuckin' night…"

[This is one of the two greatest cocktail pianist jokes I know. You'll find the other one in the James B. chapter at the end of the book.]

The best true cocktail piano story I know concerns a practical joke played by Penn Jillette. It is the perfect way to end this chapter.

Penn was in San Francisco, and he called a friend who lived in the city. The friend, unfortunately, was in a bad way. He had just split up with his girlfriend, and he was miserable. Penn suggested that they meet at The Top of the Mark, the lounge on the 19th floor of the Mark Hopkins Hotel. They could enjoy a great view of the city, and Penn could hear the details of the breakup. Penn suggested 7 p.m., and the friend agreed.

What the heartsick friend didn't know was that another of Penn's good friends was James, the cocktail pianist at The Top of the Mark. Penn called James, explained the situation, and asked James to play a special medley, starting at 7 p.m. that evening. James said sure.

That night, Penn's friend arrived at the lounge at the agreed upon time and sat down at a table. As he waited for Penn to arrive, he was serenaded with a medley of the saddest songs ever written. James pulled out all the stops: *Are You Lonesome Tonight, Ain't No Sunshine When She's Gone, Breaking Up is Hard to Do, Can't Smile Without You, Cry Me a River, Don't Let the Sun Catch you Crying, I'll Be Seeing You, It's Too Late Baby, Release Me, The Way We Were, Unchained Melody, Yesterday* – James knew them all.

Penn arrived a little late. He sat down at the table, and he and his friend started to talk. The conversation went along normally for several minutes, when suddenly the friend completely lost his cool. He slammed his hands down on the table and shouted, "What is with that fucking piano player!!"

Brilliant.

Vegas

I moved to Las Vegas in February 1998. At that time, Vegas was a city in transition, and it has changed even more in the past decade. Big corporations have taken control of the town; three corporations own most of the properties on the Strip. Whether this has been a change for the better is a matter of debate. Ask anyone who has lived in Vegas for more than thirty years, and they will tell you that it was a kinder and gentler town when the mob was in charge. Sure, every now and then someone got whacked in front of Tony Roma's rib joint, but at least a beer didn't cost seven dollars.

As I mentioned in the Introduction, I have never tried to make a living as a stand-up comedian. The one time I actually did straight stand-up comedy, I opened for a wonderful comedian named Vinnie Favorito. We worked together for eight weeks at Binion's Casino in downtown Las Vegas. Vinnie was great, and gave me excellent suggestions. I included some Vegas jokes in my set:

- Welcome to Las Vegas. How many of you brought children to Las Vegas? Really...I'm surprised. Don't bring children to Vegas. This town does not send the right message to children. Hey, I don't take hookers to Disneyland. Let's keep the two Magic Kingdoms separate.

  They did a survey. Do you know the number one reason people come to Las Vegas? It's not the gaming; it's not the entertainment; it's not the shopping; it's not the food. The number one reason people come to Las Vegas is to smoke. You can't smoke at home. We want you to smoke here. Have you seen our license plates? They say, "Nevada – California's Ashtray."

  Everywhere else you get hassled when you try to

smoke. A buddy of mine went to California to visit friends. They were having a party at their house that evening. My buddy said to the hostess, "Do you mind if I smoke?" She said, "You can't smoke in the house; go out on the patio."

So, my buddy goes outside. There's a Great Dane sprawled out on the patio. He lifts his head and sees my buddy. "Why did you have to come outside?" he asks my friend. "Did you fart?" "No, I didn't fart," my friend replies.

"Did you hump somebody's leg?" "No, I didn't hump anyone's leg."

"Did you drag your ass all over the carpet?" "No, I didn't drag my ass all over the carpet," my friend says. "I came out here to smoke a cigarette."

The dog says, "You're disgusting."

And you know, even in Las Vegas, a city that wants you to smoke, you still get hassled. Between shows last night I was standing by the escalator. I started to light up a cigarette, and a woman said to me, "You shouldn't smoke; it's bad for your health." I said, "Hey, my grandfather lived to be 103." She said, "He smoked?" I said, "No, he minded his own fucking business."

[The final joke was written by Eric Mead, who is the subject of a later chapter.]

There are many great jokes that have Las Vegas as their locale. Here are some that I've told over the years.

The Pope dies and a new Pope is elected. The new Pontiff decides to tour the United States; his itinerary includes Las Vegas. The Pope's plane lands at McCarran Airport. A welcoming committee, including Mayor Oscar Goodman waits on the tarmac. The Pope descends the stairs and Goodman begins his welcoming speech.

"Your Holiness," says the mayor, "it is a great pleasure to welcome you to...Holy Cow! Elvis! I thought you were dead." "I'ma not Elvis, I'ma da Pope," says the Pope. "Well, the resemblance is uncanny," says the mayor. "We are happy that you are here. Your limousine is waiting to take you to your hotel."

The Pope gets into the limo. The driver lowers the divider window, and turns to ask the pope for his destination. "What hotel can I take you to your...Holy Crap! Elvis! King! I thought you were dead." "I'ma not Elvis, I'ma da Pope," says the Pope. "Well, you look just like him," says the limo driver. "Where can I take you?"

The Pope is staying at the Las Vegas Hilton, and the limo driver takes him there. The Pope gets out of the limo and walks up to the front desk of the hotel. The front desk clerk says, "Yes, how may I help you? Sweet Mary and Joseph! Elvis! You're here! You're back! Just a minute, please." The clerk runs back into the executive offices. A moment later, the general manager of the Hilton comes out.

"Elvis," he says, "it is so amazing to have you back. We all thought you were dead. I've arranged for you to have your old accommodations – the presidential suite on the top floor. I've stocked the bar with booze, the refrigerator is full of food, the Jacuzzi is on, and there are four beautiful women waiting for you."

The Pope says, "Thank you. Thank you very much."

[Obviously, you say the last line á la Elvis.]

*

A man in Des Moines, Iowa wakes up in the middle of the night. He hears a little voice in his head. The voice is saying, "Go to the bank. Go to the bank." He can't clear his thoughts; the voice chants the same phrase over and over. He's unable to go back to sleep. Thinking that the only way to get rid of the voice is to follow its instruction, he goes to the bank the first thing in the morning.

As he walks up to the teller, the little voice says, "Take out all your savings. Take out all your savings." The man clears out his savings account, $30,000 in cash.

"Go to Vegas. Go to Vegas," says the voice. He takes a cab to the airport and buys a ticket for the first flight to Vegas.

When he gets off the plane, the voice says, "Go to Binion's. Go to Binion's." The man grabs a cab and heads to downtown Las Vegas, to Binion's Horseshoe Casino, which is known for taking bets of any size. When he gets to the casino, the voice says, "Go to the roulette table. Go the roulette table."

The man walks up to the first roulette table. The voice says, "Put it all on red. Put it all on red." The man puts down all his cash on red. The dealer calls over a pit boss, who approves the bet. The dealer spins the roulette wheel; he fires the ball in the opposite direction. The wheel slows; the ball bounces several times and stops...on black.

The voice says, "Aw, shit."

*

A man plays in a poker game with his buddies every Wednesday night. One evening he comes home from the game and says to his wife, "Pack your bags, you're going to live with Fred." The wife says, "What the hell are you talking about?" The man says, "I lost you to Fred in the poker game tonight." The wife says, "How could you lose me in a poker game?" The man says, "It wasn't easy; I had to fold four aces."

*

A man is gambling at a casino in North Las Vegas. He has a terrible streak of bad luck, and he loses everything; he is completely tapped out. He goes into the men's room to relieve himself, and discovers that it costs a quarter to use the stalls. He walks back out into the casino and accosts a man walking by.

"Listen," he says, "I'm really embarrassed about this, but I need to use the restroom and I don't even have a quarter to get in a stall. Can I bum a quarter from you?" The stranger gives the man a quarter, and he goes back into the restroom. He discovers that someone has left the door to one of the stalls ajar. He goes in without paying, does his business, and walks back out into the casino. He looks for the man who gave him the quarter, but he can't find him, so he puts the quarter into a slot machine. He hits three 7s, and wins a hundred dollars.

The man takes the money to a five-dollar blackjack table. He plays for a few hours, and wins almost a thousand dollars. He takes that money to the roulette table, puts it all on red, and wins. He lets it ride and wins again. In an hour, he has $50,000. He goes to the craps table, and in two hours has won $250,000. He goes into the high stakes room and sits down at the baccarat table. By dawn he has won one million dollars.

The man flies back home and uses his money to start a business. His enterprise is amazingly successful, and after a year is worth two hundred million dollars. *Forbes* magazine names him the entrepreneur of the year. The man's home town holds a big ceremony honoring him. At the ceremony, the man tells the story of his amazing luck in Vegas, and how a quarter changed his life.

"I owe it all to one man," he tells the crowd. "If I could ever find him I would share my fortune with him." A fellow in the crowd raises his hand. "It was me," he says. "I was the one who gave you the quarter."

"No, I meant the guy who left the stall door open."

*

A man and his wife are visiting Las Vegas. They've gone to bed, but the man can't sleep. He puts on some clothes and goes down to the casino. He has five dollars in his pocket, and he puts it on red at the roulette table. He wins and lets the bet ride. He wins again. He wins ten times in a row.

He takes that money and goes to the blackjack table. He plays for two hours and walks away with $20,000. He goes to the craps table and makes sixteen consecutive passes. He's won $250,000. He lets it all ride on the Pass line. He rolls the dice and craps out, losing everything.

He goes back up to his hotel room, slips into his pajamas, and gets into bed. His wife stirs, and says to him, "Where were you?" He says, "I couldn't sleep, so I went down to the casino to gamble." "How did you do?" she asks. "I lost five dollars."

*

Q: How do you make 150 lovely, gray-haired grandmothers say, "shit?"
A: Yell, "Bingo!"

*

It's Saturday night, and the Bellagio buffet is jammed with diners. Suddenly, a woman stands up and screams, "Help me! My son has swallowed a quarter and he's choking to death." Several people come to the boy's aid. They pound him on the back and attempt the Heimlich maneuver, but the quarter remains firmly lodged in the boy's throat. The boy is about to lose consciousness when a man at a nearby table stands up and says to the woman, "Don't worry, I have experience with this." So saying, he reaches down, grabs the boy's crotch, and squeezes. The quarter shoots out of his mouth and lands on the table.

"That was amazing," says the mother. "Are you a paramedic?" "No," says the man, "I work for the I.R.S."

I often tell the next joke as if it actually happened to me, so that's the way I'll tell it to you.

- I was walking out of the Riviera casino the other night. It was about one in the morning, and this stranger walks up to me. You know how we all have a comfort zone perimeter that extends about a foot and a half around us? Well, this guy stepped inside that, getting a little bit into my personal space. I didn't feel threatened, but it was a little disconcerting.

"You don't know me, and I don't know you," he said, "but you look like you might be a nice guy. My wife is very sick. She has to take these pills every day. They are very expensive, and if she doesn't take them she'll die. The pills cost $500 a month. So what I'm wondering is, will you give me $500 so I can buy my wife the pills?"

"Gosh," I said, "I don't want to be a schmuck here; I'm not unsympathetic to your problem. I'm just afraid that if I gave you the $500 you'd turn right around, walk back into the casino, and gamble it away."

"Oh, no," he replied, "I've got gambling money..."

And finally, here's a joke that epitomizes living in Las Vegas.

A man dies and goes to heaven. St. Peter tells him that because of a clerical error he will have to spend a few days in hell until his paperwork is processed. There is a flash of light, and the man finds himself in hell. A raucous party is in full swing all around him. Loud rock music blares; people are dancing wildly; alcohol flows freely; there are tables brimming with fine food as far as the eye can see. Beautiful women are everywhere. People are gambling and carousing. The man spends the next three days partying like he has never partied before.

Just then, there is a flash of light, and the man finds himself back in heaven. St. Peter shows him around. A group of people are singing Gregorian chants. Other people are resting on puffy clouds, reading books of poetry. The air is filled with the sounds of harp music. After three days, the man is bored stiff. He finds St. Peter and says, "Listen, if it's all the same to you, I'd like to go back to hell." "It's your choice," says St. Peter, and the man disappears in a flash of light.

When the man reappears in hell, he finds himself chained to a large rock in front of an enormous blast furnace. A heavy shovel is attached to his hands. The heat is overwhelming. For what seems an eternity, he shovels coal into the furnace as little imps dance around him, sticking him in the ass with tiny pitchforks.

One day, Satan walks by, and the man yells out to him. "Hey, what's going on here? When I came down here before there was dancing, and booze, and women, and gambling, and fun. Now I'm shoveling coal into a blast furnace. What's the deal?"

Satan replies, "Well, the first time you were a visitor. Now you're a local."

One nice thing about moving to Las Vegas was that so many of my friends live here. The town is full of magicians. In fact, you can hardly spit without hitting a magician. (Although it's fun to try, especially from the observation deck of the Stratosphere.) One of my great delights of the past ten years has been the opportunity to spend time with Johnny and Pam Thompson. Johnny is one of the magic world's living treasures. He is one of the few magicians on the planet who is an expert at stage, parlor, and close-up magic. He is a walking encyclopedia of magical knowledge; I have worked with Johnny as a consultant to several well-known magicians and I am always amazed at the amount of detailed, arcane, useful information he has filed away in his memory banks.

Johnny and Pam are also truly funny people, and each of them possesses exquisite comedy timing. Their stage act, known as Tomsoni & Company, is a brilliant combination of virtuoso magical technique and slapstick comedy. Johnny performs miracles, and Pam (as his bored assistant) could not care less. They are as funny offstage as on. Johnny and I share several common bonds. He is an excellent musician (he played with the Harmonicats), and we had the same mentor, a man named Harry Riser.

Johnny surrounds himself with talented and funny friends. One night, at a dinner party, Johnny's friend Artie Schroeck (a composer, arranger, and jazz vibes player) told one of the best animal jokes I'd ever heard.

> A man sees an ad in the paper offering a Great Dane for sale. The price is quite low, so the man calls the owner and sets up a time to see the dog. The man knocks on the owner's door, and is invited inside. "Can I take a look at the dog?" asks the man. "Sure," says

the owner. He leads the man into the den, where a beautiful Great Dane lies sleeping in front of the fireplace.

The man checks the dog's eyes, looks in his ears, examines his teeth, and feels the dog's haunches. The dog is in excellent health. The man asks the owner, "Why are you selling the dog?" The owner replies, "Ask the dog about his life as a dog." The man is puzzled, but says to the dog, "Tell me about your life as a dog."

The dog sits up and looks attentively at the man. "Well," the dog says, "I've had a most interesting life. I'm one of the few dogs who has gone to college; I received my M.B.A. degree from Harvard. I wrote a book about my life as a dog, titled, coincidentally, *My Life as a Dog*. It was on the *New York Times* best-seller list for twenty weeks. In the past few months I've been negotiating several movie deals, the most interesting being a deal with Disney. They want me to star in a remake of *Rin Tin Tin*; of course, I'll be playing him as a Great Dane, rather than a German Shepard. All in all, I've had a most interesting and satisfying life."

The man is dumbfounded. He says to the owner, "This is unbelievable! Why in the world are you selling this dog?"

The owner replies, "Because he's a fucking liar!"

The reference to Harvard in the above joke reminded me of this one...

A fellow from Kentucky receives a scholarship to Harvard. He's walking around Cambridge trying to find the campus. He spots a man sitting on a park bench reading a newspaper.

"Excuse me," the Kentuckian says to the man, "can you tell me where Harvard is at?"

The man lowers his newspaper and looks at the Kentuckian with disdain. "My mother told me never to speak to anyone who ends his sentence with a preposition."

"Sorry," says the Kentuckian. "Could you tell me where Harvard is at, asshole?"

...and the reference to Disney reminded me of this one.

Mickey Mouse is consulting with a lawyer. "According to your affidavit," the lawyer says to Mickey, "you want a divorce from Minnie Mouse because she's crazy."

"No sir," says Mickey. "I didn't say she was crazy; I said she was fucking Goofy!"

Johnny and Pam's onstage confrontational dynamic always reminds me of the great relationship jokes I've heard. Let's start with one that has a gambling theme.

A man calls his wife at home. "Honey, pack your bags," he says. "I've just won the lottery."

"Where are we going?" asks the wife.

"I don't care where you go," says the husband, "as long as your fat ass is gone by the time I get home."

*

A man is convinced that his wife is cheating on him. One day he comes home from work several hours early. He storms into his apartment and immediately smells cigar smoke. His wife is in bed with the covers pulled up around her neck. The husband rushes to the window and sees a man running to get into a car that's parked in front of the apartment building.

In a blind rage the husband runs into the kitchen, lifts the refrigerator, carries it to the window, and tosses it out. The refrigerator falls ten stories and lands on the man getting in the car, killing him instantly. Unfortunately, the strain of lifting the refrigerator is too much for the husband's heart; he has a massive heart attack and dies.

The husband awakes and finds himself in front of the Pearly Gates. Two other men are standing with him.

St. Peter appears. He says to the husband, "Why are you here?" "I was convinced that my wife was cheating on me. I came home from work early and caught her naked in bed. When I looked out the window I saw her lover running for his car. I lifted the refrigerator and threw it out the window. The strain was too great for me; I had a heart attack and died."

"Why are you here?" St. Peter asks the second man. "It must have been some sort of fluke accident," the man replies. "I had just gone into my apartment building when I realized that I had left my cell phone in the car. I ran back outside to get it, and as I was opening the car door something really big hit me. The next thing I knew, I was up here."

"Why are you here?" St. Peter asks the third man. "I have no idea," he replies. "I was just sitting in a refrigerator, minding my own business..."

*

A man comes home early from work and catches his wife in bed with his best friend. He throws the wife out of the bedroom and says to his friend, "Bad dog. Bad dog."

*

Two friends meet on the street. One of them is sporting two fresh black eyes. "Holy smoke," says one. "Who gave you the black eyes?" "My wife," says the other. "I thought she was out of town," says the first man. The second replies, "So did I."

*

A man is working at his office one afternoon when he's hit with a terrible headache. The pain is intense. The man's secretary walks in and sees that he is obviously in discomfort. He tells the secretary about the headache. "I have a surefire cure for a headache," the secretary tells him. "I don't live far from here. Give me twenty minutes, and then come over to my apartment." She writes down the address and leaves. The man finishes up what work he can and drives over to the secretary's apartment.

He rings the bell, and the secretary opens the door. She is wearing the flimsiest of negligees, and holds two aspirin and a glass of water. The man takes the aspirin, tosses down a mouthful of water, and immediately falls in lust. He picks up the secretary, carries her to the bedroom, and they make passionate love. When they finish, the man falls into a deep sleep.

When he awakes, it is 11:30 in the evening. The secretary is panicked. "I tried to wake you up," she says, "but I couldn't rouse you. Your wife is going to kill you." "It's okay," says the man, "I know what to do. Bring me some talcum power." The secretary brings the man the powder. He rubs it over his hands and heads home.

When he arrives home he finds that his wife has locked him out of the house. He pounds on the door and rings the doorbell until his wife opens the door. "Listen, I can explain," the man says to his wife. "This afternoon at work I was hit with a terrible headache. My secretary said she had a surefire cure, so I went over to her apartment. When she came to the door she was wearing a flimsy negligee and was holding two aspirin. I took the aspirin and I was overwhelmed by passion. I carried her to her bedroom and we made love for several hours. Then I fell asleep and just woke up a few minutes ago. I drove straight home."

The wife looks at the man skeptically. "Wait a minute," she says. "Let me see your hands." Sheepishly, the man holds out his hands. "I knew it, you lying bastard," says the wife, "you were bowling again."

*

A woman's husband has just left for work when there's a knock at the door. A nicely dressed man is standing on the front stoop. The woman opens the door. "I'm sorry to disturb you," says the man, "but do you have a vagina?" The woman is shocked and outraged. She slams the door in the man's face, runs upstairs, and locks herself in her bedroom.

The next day, at about 9 a.m., there is a knock at the door. It's the same man. The woman opens the door. "I really am sorry to bother you," says the man, "but do you have a vagina?" The woman is completely freaked out. She slams the door, pulls the curtains closed, shuts off all the lights, runs upstairs, locks her bedroom door, and hides under the bed.

When her husband comes home from work that evening the woman tells him about the rude man who has been knocking on the door. "He's vulgar and obnoxious, and he scares me," says the woman. "It will all be okay," says the husband. "Tomorrow, when I leave for work, I'll only drive one street over. I'll park the car and come inside through the patio door. Then I'll hide behind the front door. If the man knocks, I want you to answer the door. If he says anything vulgar, I'll jump out and pound him."

The next morning, the husband leaves, sneaks back into the house, and hides behind the front door. At 9 a.m., there is a knock at the door. It is the same man. The wife answers the door. "Excuse me again," says the man. "I'm sorry to be a bother. Do you have a vagina?" "Yes," says the woman defiantly, "I have a vagina." "In that case," replies the man, "would you please tell your husband to stop fucking my wife?"

*

The man with the worst foot odor problem in the world has a date with a woman who has the worst halitosis in the world. He meets her at her apartment. She grabs her purse, and says, "Are you ready to go?" "In just a minute," says the man. He goes into the bathroom, takes off his shoes, throws his socks in the corner, washes his feet in the tub, rubs medicated powder on them, puts on a fresh pair of socks, puts his shoes back on, and walks back into the living room.

"Are you ready to go?" he asks. "In just a minute," says the woman. She runs into the bathroom, brushes her teeth, gargles twice with a strong mouthwash, and pops a breath freshener into her mouth. She walks back out into the living room.

"Listen," she says to the man, "before we leave there's something I need to tell you."

"I know," says the man. "You ate my socks."

*

A man and a woman meet at a bar. They really hit it off, and after a few hours they go back to the woman's apartment. They are making out passionately as they make their way through the living room into the woman's bedroom. The bedroom is full of stuffed animals; they are everywhere – on the bed, on the dresser, and stacked up on bookshelves. The couple clears a space on the bed and they make passionate love.

When they finish, the man says to the woman, "So, how was I?"

She says, "You can take something off the bottom shelf."

[This is, of course, a carny joke. You could change the punch line to "You can take something off the top shelf," but if you tell the joke to a carny (and I know a few), you'll get a bigger laugh telling it as written.]

*

A man is sitting watching a football game. He says to his wife, "Get me a beer." She says, "Get your own damn beer." He says, "I told you to get me a beer." She replies, "I'm not getting you a beer. Get off the couch and get it yourself." He says to her, "If you don't get me a beer right now, you're not going to see me for three days." She says, "I'm not getting you a beer."

Sure enough, the first day the woman doesn't see her husband. She doesn't see him on the second day. By the third day the swelling has gone down enough that she can open one eye...

[This is not a politically correct joke, so use it at your own risk. It did, however, get a big laugh when I did a gig at Tempura House, a halfway house for lightly battered women.]

*

- A man is fed up with his wife's extravagant spending habits. "I'm tired of the way you spend money," he tells her, "so I'm cutting you off. You can spend money on things we need to run the house, but nothing else."

"Fine," says the wife. "In that case I'll go out and make my own money." "What in the world are you going to do to make money?" asks the husband. "I'll be a hooker," says the wife. The husband wishes her luck, and she storms out the door.

The wife doesn't return until 4 a.m. the next morning. The husband is sitting in the living room waiting for her. "So, how did it go?" he asks her. "It went great," she says. "I made $20.25."

"Twenty-five cents?" says the husband. "Who gave you a quarter?"

"Everybody."

*

Two women are chatting in front of their houses. A delivery truck pulls up and the delivery man presents one of the ladies with a large bouquet of roses. "Oh, great," says the woman, "they're from my husband. Now I'll have to spend the weekend on my back with my legs in the air."

"What's the problem?" says her friend. "You don't own a vase?"

The last joke of this chapter is one of my favorites to tell in front of a big group. What is remarkable about it is not that it gets a big laugh (it's a funny joke), but that it gets two completely different laughs. The men are laughing at one thing, and the women are laughing at another.

A man has been unable to perform sexually in his marriage. He goes to a doctor for a consultation. "It's never a good thing to have a problem like this," says the doctor, "but if you *have* to have this problem, now is a good time to have it. Medical technology has advanced to the point where there are a number of viable options available.

"For $5,000 we can do a basic surgical repair procedure. At the end of the operation, you'll be able to have sex once a month. However, for $15,000, we can do more extensive surgery; when the recovery period is over you can have sex once a week.

"But I should also tell you that there is a new, cutting-edge, micro-surgical procedure available. It costs $30,000, but after the recovery period it's as if you're brand new. You can have sex as often as you'd like. Which procedure do you want?"

"Well," says the man, "I should talk it over with my wife." "Of course you should," says the doctor. "Please come back when you've made your decision."

The fellow returns to the doctor's office the next day. "So," says the doctor, "what did you decide?"

"We're going to remodel the kitchen."

Jay

Jay Marshall was one of the finest variety artists of the last half of the 20th century. He was a magician, a ventriloquist, a puppeteer, and a comedian. He played the Palladium Theatre in London on many occasions, and appeared often on the *Ed Sullivan Show*. He had a love of all things related to show business, and during his lifetime accumulated an enormous collection of (for lack of a better word) stuff – books, posters, props, records, sheet music, ephemera, on a wide variety of subjects. He knew and had stories about most of the important and not so important magicians of his day. He saw Harry Houdini perform. (Jay was six years old at the time and he fell asleep during the show.) With Jay as a friend, you achieved one degree of separation from almost anybody you could think of.

Jay and his wife Francis owned and ran Magic, Inc., a magic shop on the north side of Chicago. That's where I first met him. I was in my early teens, and my family had taken a trip to Chicago (I don't remember why). The magic shop was nowhere near where we were going, but I cajoled my father into making a side trip there. I knew who Jay Marshall was; I had read about him in *The Phoenix*, a magic magazine published in the 1940s and 50s. (By this time I had become a magic book junkie, ordering everything I could afford from Stoner's shop. A hardbound reprint of *The Phoenix* had been published by Tannen's Magic Company.) I was too in awe of Jay to say anything to him; I don't even remember if I bought anything – there were far too many books and props on display to decide on any one item.

I got to know Jay personally in 1973 when he visited the home of Harry Riser, the man who was instrumental in my magical development. Jay was in Indianapolis to watch the first weekend of qualifications at the Indy 500. We became friends, and I would occasionally drive up to Chicago to visit him; we'd take in some jazz clubs, and we'd watch Heba Haba Al Andrucci perform his hysterical bar magic at the New York Lounge, which was down the street from Jay's shop.

In 1976, Jay reduced me to helpless laughter by giving me a private performance of his "Salute" routine at 1 a.m. in the lobby of a hotel in Evansville, Indiana. This was a routine that was part of the act Jay performed for servicemen during World War II. Jay and I were attending the annual convention of the International Brotherhood of Magicians (I.B.M.). Four years later, I worked with Jay for the first time at this same convention, which, coincidentally, was held again in Evansville. We were part of a mid-morning cabaret show. My jazz trio was providing music for the show. Jay gave us a lovely introduction: "It's great to have Mike Close and the band with us this morning. Normally, they don't stop puking until noon."

Jay was one of the best joke tellers I've ever heard. Not only was his repertoire endless, but he had jokes that I've never heard anyone else tell. (Jay was the guy who told Gershon Legman, author of *Rationale of the Dirty Joke*, the Aristocrats joke.) Here are a few of them.

> The year is 1993. The Detroit Lions are having a miserable season; their offense is completely ineffective. One day, the head coach gets a phone call from one of his scouts. The scout has discovered a Bosnian soldier who can throw a hand grenade into a barrel from one hundred yards away. Even though the Bosnian War is in full force, the coach flies to Sarajevo to watch the soldier in action.
>
> The coach and the scout meet the soldier at his barracks. They walk out to an open field and the soldier gives a demonstration. Sure enough, he is amazingly accurate, even when throwing while at a dead run. "Have you ever thrown an American football?" asks the coach. "No," says the soldier, "but I'll give it a try." The soldier is just as accurate with a football. "Do you know anything about American football?" asks the

coach. "No," says the soldier. "We'll teach you," says the coach, and he makes arrangements for the soldier to come to America.

Back in Detroit, the soldier is given a crash course in how to quarterback a football team. The next Sunday, he starts the game. He's amazing. The Lions win the game 56-21; every point scored by the Lions was the result of a long, unerringly accurate pass by the soldier.

The team is jubilant; they carry the soldier off the field on their shoulders. There is rejoicing in the locker room. It takes a few moments before the coach can get a word with his new quarterback. "You were sensational," says the coach. "Is there anything I can do for you?" "Yes," says the soldier, "I'd like to call my mother and tell her about the game." The coach brings a phone to the soldier and he makes the call.

"Hi, Mom," says the soldier. "I want to tell you about the football game today." "It's all your fault," says the mother. "What's my fault?" asks the soldier.

"Men came into the house today," his mother says. "They dragged your father outside and beat him senseless. Your sister was nearly raped on her way home from school. The houses on either side of us are on fire; I may have to hang up in case the fire spreads to our house. And it's all your fault."

"How is it my fault?" asks the soldier.

"You're the one who made us move to Detroit."

*

A man walks into a diner. There's a sign on the counter that says, "Special Today – Banjo Sandwich." The fellow asks the counterman, "What's a Banjo Sandwich?" "It's good," says the counterman, "you should try one." So, the man orders the Banjo Sandwich.

The counterman brings the food. The sandwich consists of two medium poached eggs on two slices of white bread, with a little mayonnaise. "What makes this a Banjo Sandwich?" asks the man. "Try it," says the counterman. So the man takes a big bite of the sandwich and goes: "Ooh." [This part is visual. Using both hands, you mime taking a bite of the sandwich. The left hand moves away to the left (holding the imaginary sandwich) as the right hand brushes off the imaginary egg yolk that has dropped onto the front of your shirt. The action looks exactly as if you are playing the banjo.]

Jay had another great visual gag that he often used when he was the emcee of a show.

A Jewish fellow is walking through New York City carrying two large watermelons, one underneath each arm. [Mime this position.] Another man stops the Jewish fellow. "Excuse me," he asks, "do you know how to get to Rockefeller Center?"

[The next part is all mime. Get down on your knees, and (with some degree of effort) place each imaginary watermelon on the ground. Then, look up and shrug your shoulders.]

*

Jesus has been in heaven for a little while, and St. Peter asks him to check people through the Pearly Gates so he can take a coffee break. Jesus takes over the job, and as he is admitting people he sees an old blind man. The man looks very familiar. When he reaches the front of the line, Jesus speaks to him. "Excuse me, old man," he says. "I think I recognize you. Where did you live back on earth?" "I lived in the Mediterranean area," replies the old man.

"What was your name?" Jesus asks. "In my country, I was called Joseph."

"What did you do for a living?" "I was a carpenter, a woodcarver, a craftsman," replies the old man.

"Did you have any children?" asks Jesus. "I had a son," the man replies. "At least, some people said he was my son, but I lost him."

"Father," says Jesus, embracing him. "Pinocchio!" says the old man.

*

Joseph and Mary are traveling from Nazareth to Bethlehem. They are near their destination when their cart is stopped by a suspicious Roman guard. The guard looks at the two of them and suddenly gets an intuitive flash.

"You're from Nazareth, aren't you" says the guard. "That's right," says Joseph.

"And you're traveling to Bethlehem." "Yes," says Joseph.

"Your name is Joseph, her name is Mary, and she's going to have a baby," says the soldier. "Yes."

"And when the baby is born, you will name him Jesus." Joseph replies, "Do we look Puerto Rican?"

*

A man owns a pit bull; the dog is aggressive, barking, snarling, and chasing anyone who walks by the man's house. The situation has gotten so bad that the mailman tosses the man's mail onto the sidewalk, the UPS man leaves his deliveries on the curb, and the paperboy races by the house on his bicycle, often wildly throwing the man's newspaper on the roof.

The man takes the dog to the vet in an attempt to solve the problem. "We have found," says the vet, "that neutering an animal calms them down substantially, eliminating almost all aggressive tendencies." The man has the dog neutered, and the operation seems to have the desired result – the dog now sleeps peacefully on the front porch.

The man informs the UPS man and the postman that the dog is no longer a threat, but the paperboy continues to race by the house, throwing the newspaper randomly as he passes. Finally, the man is able to halt the paperboy before he flies by.

"You don't have to worry about the dog anymore," the man tells the paperboy. "I had him neutered." "You had him what?" asks the paperboy. "I had him neutered; the veterinarian removed his testicles."

"Gosh, mister," says the paperboy, "you should have just pulled his teeth. I wasn't afraid of getting fucked."

*

The Amazing Randi is in San Francisco speaking in front of a group of people who study paranormal psychology. "Let's get a little information before we start," says Randi. "How many of you know someone who has seen a ghost?" Almost every hand in the room goes up. "How many of you have personally experienced some type of paranormal phenomena?" About half the people in the auditorium raise their hands. "How many of you have personally seen a ghost?" Twenty people raise their hands. "And for the sake of completeness, how many of you have had sex with a ghost?" One man raises his hand. Since Randi had meant the last question to be a joke, he is intrigued.

"You've had sex with a ghost?" he asks the man. The man nods his head in agreement. "Would you please come up here and tell the group about it?" The man runs up on stage.

The fellow is East Indian, and he immediately launches into his story. "I remember it very much as if it were just yesterday," he begins. "It was the middle of the afternoon, and I was standing on a street in downtown New Delhi. I looked across the street, and through the hustle and bustle of the traffic, I could see it. And for some reason, I was very attracted to it. So, I waited for the minutest break in the traffic, and then, quick like a bunny, I ran across the street to it. I unzipped my trousers, and we did it."

"Wait a minute, wait a minute" says Randi. "You're telling me that in the middle of the afternoon, on a busy street in New Delhi, you had sex with a ghost?"

"Oh, no, no, no," says the man. "I thought you said *goat*."

[This is one of three Indian dialect jokes that I tell all the time. The other two are coming up next. The second joke is a fine variation of the one above, and the third joke is one of the greatest jokes I've ever told.]

I always tell the following joke as if it happened to me.

> Since moving to Las Vegas, I've become obsessed thinking about fate. It doesn't make any sense to me. How could it be that one person puts three dollars into the Megabucks slot machine and wins millions of dollars when another person gets on an airplane that flies into a mountain? I needed to find out what the meaning of fate was.
>
> So, I made a pilgrimage to India. I trekked through a desert, climbed a high mountain, and made my way to the back of a dark cave. There sat a wizened old man with a long beard – the guru. I asked him, "What is the meaning of fate?"
>
> He said to me, "There is a designated time, and there is a designated place. You must arrive at the place at the designated time. If you do so, it will be there. Should it not be there, you must leave the place, and come back at a later time. Then it will be there."
>
> I said to him, "That's the meaning of fate?"
>
> "Oh, no," he replied, "I thought you said *freight*."

*

A man from New Delhi has been living in the United States for a year. Lately, he hasn't been feeling very well. The man phones his doctor. "There is something very, very wrong with me," he tells the doctor. "I have pounding, throbbing migraine headaches, bouts of nausea, stiffness in my joints, heaviness in my extremities, fullness as if there is a great bowling ball lodged in my stomach, lack of energy, and a general feeling of malaise."

"Wow," says the doctor. "Is there a grocery store near you?" "Yes," says the Indian. "Okay, go to the grocery store and buy the freshest chicken you can find. Put the raw chicken in a brown paper bag. Roll up the top of the bag and put the bag in your backyard in the sun for a week. Then give me a call." There is a long pause, and then the Indian says, "Okay."

A week goes by, and the Indian calls the doctor. "Listen," he says, "I have done as you requested, but there have been no improvements to any of my conditions. I doubt the effectiveness of your prescribed treatment." "Oh, we're not done yet," says the doctor. "Go out to your backyard. Unroll the top of the bag. I want you to pee in the bag and I want you to poop in the bag. Then roll up the top of bag and leave it in your backyard in the sun for a week." There is a long pause, and then the Indian says, "Okay."

Another week goes by, and the Indian calls the doctor. "I fear your treatment is useless," he says. "I feel worse than I have ever felt in my life. I could barely muster the strength to punch the digits of your phone number." "We're almost done," says the doctor. "I want you to go into your backyard, unroll the top of the bag, stick your head in the bag, and stay like that for an hour. Then call me back." There is a very long pause, and then the Indian says, "Okay."

An hour passes, and the doctor gets a phone call. It's the Indian. "This is amazing. This is a miracle. I am cured," he gushes. "I feel completely rejuvenated. I feel like a sixteenyear-old boy." "I knew it," says the doctor.

"What was wrong with me?" asks the Indian.

"You were homesick."

[You need to pick your audience carefully, but I'll tell you, I've hurt people with this joke. You just can't see the punch line coming. It is one of a rare group of jokes whose punch line occurs on the final word. (The Bosnia soldier joke is one of these.) When I first started to tell this joke, I needed to warm up my Indian accent. I did this by remembering Richard Libertini as Prahka Lasa in the movie *All of Me*. ("Back in bowl. Back in bowl.") Don't leave out any of the details; they make the joke work.]

*

Three British soldiers have fought gallantly in the Falkland Islands War. They have returned to their army base in Britain, and are to receive a special tribute from the base Captain. "Men," says the Captain, "the company has set aside a special fund to specifically reward heroism in battle. It is a monetary reward, and the way we distribute it is unique. The company will give you ten pounds for every inch between any two of your body parts that you nominate."

A slim, tall Lieutenant says, "Measure from the top of my head to the base of my heel, sir!" The captain measures him. He's six feet, five inches tall. "Lieutenant, you measure out at seventy-seven inches; I'm pleased to present you with 770 pounds."

A lanky Sergeant says, "Measure from the tip of my left middle finger to the tip of my right middle finger, arms outstretched, sir!" The Sergeant isn't tall, but he has long arms. The Captain measures him. "Sergeant, your arm span measures five feet, eleven inches. I'm pleased to present you with 710 pounds."

One soldier remains. "Where would you like to be measured Corporal?" asks the Captain. "From the tip of my penis to my testicles, sir!" says the Corporal. "Uh, that's an unusual request, but very well, Corporal, drop your trousers."

The Captain places one end of the tape measure at the tip of the Corporal's penis and extends the tape measure along it. He stops suddenly. "My god, Corporal, where are your testicles?"

"Goose Green, Falklands, sir!"

*

A Greek restaurant and a Chinese restaurant are next door to each other on Rush Street in Chicago. The owner of the Greek restaurant delights in teasing the owner of the Chinese restaurant about his inability to pronounce certain English words.

> The Greek owner takes some people to lunch at the Chinese restaurant. The Chinese owner waits on them. "We'll take some hot and sour soup, some beef and broccoli, some cashew chicken, and this. What's this item here?" asks the Greek owner. "That's flied lice," says the Chinese owner. The Greek and his friends roar with laughter.
>
> The Chinese man gets fed up with being ridiculed by the Greek. He takes a week off work and spends the time practicing English. For twelve hours a day he repeats the words that give him trouble. On the Monday that he returns to the restaurant, the Greek owner brings some friends in for lunch. The Chinese man waits on them.
>
> "We'll have some egg drop soup," says the Greek owner, "some lemon chicken, some moo goo gai pan, and some of this. What's this item here?"
>
> "That's fried rice, fried rice, fried rice," says Chinese owner. "How do like that, you Gleek plick?"

And that reminds me of these two jokes.

> A Chinese couple is lying in bed at midnight. The man turns to his wife and says, "How about a little 69?"
>
> She says, "Why you want moo shu pork at this time of night?"

*

> A couple is having dinner at a Chinese restaurant. They finish the meal and the waiter comes up to them. "How was your food?" he asks. "The chicken was rubbery," says the man. The waiter says, "Ah, thank you very much."

Here are a couple more jokes I remember Jay telling.

> A man serves in the army during World War II. At the end of the war he is stationed in Paris, awaiting his discharge. He has few duties, so he spends his days wandering through the City of Light. One evening, he

finds himself in front of a small bistro halfway down a narrow side street. The man is hungry, so he goes in to have dinner.

He orders his meal, and then notices a table tent. It reads, "For your entertainment pleasure, the Amazing André will perform tableside. By request only. Twenty-five francs." The man has an excellent and enjoyable meal. He orders a cup of coffee and asks the waiter to send over the Amazing André.

A distinguished-looking man wearing a tailored tuxedo walks up to the table. He has dark black hair and a pencil-thin moustache. "I am the Amazing André," he announces. "Did you wish to see the show?" "Absolutely," says the man.

André places a walnut on the edge of the table. He unzips his fly and removes an enormous erection. He slams the erection down on the walnut, neatly splitting it in half. He then steps back from the table and readjusts his clothing. The man is stunned. He gives André his fee, and tips him another twenty-five francs. André leaves; the man pays for his meal and returns to his barracks.

The man is discharged from the army and returns to his home in Chicago. He gets a job at an insurance company. He works for the company for forty years, eventually becoming a senior vice-president. At his retirement party, the company presents him with an all-expense-paid trip for two to Paris. He has not been to Paris since his army days and is delighted at the prospect of showing his wife around the city.

He and his wife travel to Paris, and they have a wonderful time wandering through the city, seeing the sites. One evening they find themselves on a small side street that feels very familiar to the man. They walk down it, and, about halfway down the street, they find the little bistro that the man had visited so many years before.

They go into the restaurant and order dinner. The man notices a table tent. It reads, "For your entertainment pleasure, the Amazing André will perform tableside.

By request only. Two hundred francs." The man can't believe it. "That's impossible," he thinks. "André was in his forties when I saw him. It can't be the same guy."

After dinner, the man asks the waiter to send André over to perform. Sure enough, it is the same man. His hair and moustache are now steel gray, but he is extremely fit, and he walks with the gait of a much younger man. "I am the Amazing André," he announces. "Do you wish to see the show?" "Absolutely," say the man and wife simultaneously.

André places a coconut on the edge of the table. He unzips his fly and removes an enormous erection. "André, André, André," says the man. "A coconut?"

"Ah," says André, "the eyes are the first thing to go."

*

A man who is extremely self-centered goes to a psychiatrist for treatment. "So, Mr. Jones," says the psychiatrist, "tell me why you have come to me." "I'm a self-centered egotist," says Jones. "I care about no one but myself. I've been fired from four high-paying jobs because of my egotistical attitude. I can't maintain a relationship. I'm estranged from my parents and my siblings. I've been married and divorced four times. Right now, I'm seeing a wonderful woman, and I know that I'll ruin things because I'm so self centered. I need help."

"This is good," says the doctor. "The fact that you realize that you have a problem is the first step on the road to recovery. Why don't you lie down on the couch and we'll talk a bit." Mr. Jones gets comfortable on the couch.

"Tell me this," says the doctor, "do you have any hobbies? A hobby would show an interest away from self, and would be a positive thing." "Yes," says Jones, "I do have a hobby. I keep bees." "Excellent," says the psychiatrist. "Tell me about it."

"Well, I have about 10,000 bees in a shoebox in my

closet." "You have 10,000 bees in a shoebox?" says the doctor. "They'll smother!"

"Fuck 'em."

*

Seeking a more spiritual and serene life, a man joins a monastery. The monastery has a strict policy on talking: the apprentice monks are only allowed to say two words every year on the anniversary of the day they joined.

The man settles into life in the monastery; he prays, he studies, and he tends his garden. On the anniversary of the day he joined, he goes into the head monk's office. "Bad food," he says, and he leaves.

Another year goes by. The man prays, studies, and tends his garden. On his anniversary day he goes into the head monk's office. "Uncomfortable bed," he says, and he leaves.

Another year passes, with the man maintaining the same routine. It is his third anniversary at the monastery. He walks into the head monk's office. "I quit," he says.

"Well, you might as well," says the head monk. "You've done nothing but bitch since you got here."

*

A retired actor who is living in Florida gets a call from an agent in New York City. "I have a great opportunity for you," the agent says. "If you can get on a plane to New York this morning, I can put you into a show this evening. It's a very small part, but it's an important part. You only have one line of dialogue. At the beginning of the second act you walk out and say, 'Hark, I hear the cannon's roar!' I realize you haven't worked for a while, but this could be the start of a comeback for you. Will you do it?" "Sure," says the actor.

The actor races to the airport and gets on the next flight to New York. During his trip he rehearses various ways to deliver the line. Should it be "*Hark*...I hear the cannon's roar," or "Hark, I hear the *cannon's* roar," or "Hark, *I* hear the cannon's roar." He agonizes over these possibilities during the cab ride to the theater and as he is being fitted for his costume.

The play starts; the actor paces backstage, practicing his line. He has decided that the line should build in intensity to the word "roar." The first act ends. During the intermission the actor changes his mind, and decides that the line should be delivered in a pensive way, reflecting on the horror of war. The audience has returned to their seats. The curtain opens for the second act.

The actor walks out on stage. There is an enormous "BOOM."

He turns and says, "What the fuck was that?"

To me, the story above is the archetypical Jay Marshall joke; I heard him tell it many times. There is also a story (possibly apocryphal) concerning this joke: Jay was spending the Fourth of July holiday at the home of his friend Tommy Edwards. It was a warm afternoon, and Jay had fallen asleep in a lawn chair in the backyard. Someone lit a firecracker and tossed it under Jay's chair. It exploded. Jay sat up and said, "Hark, I hear the cannon's roar."

Jay and I attended many magic conventions together. Often at these conventions, the theater where the evening shows were presented was some distance from the convention hotel. I told Jay that whenever I had a car, I would drive him to and from the theater, so he wouldn't have to ride in a crowded bus with the other conventioneers.

In 1994, we were in Orlando, Florida, at another I.B.M. convention. I had heard a variation of the "Hark, I hear the cannon's roar" joke, and I was eager to tell it to Jay. Here's the joke.

An actor in New York City is getting on in years, and he no longer gets work because he has trouble memorizing dialogue. One day, he gets a phone call from a Broadway producer. "Listen," the producer says, "if you can remember one line of dialogue, and you can get down here for a costume fitting, I can put you in a play this evening. Can you do that; can you remember one lousy line of dialogue?" "I can," says the actor. "No problem at all."

"Here's all you have to do," says the producer. "At the beginning of the second act of the play you walk out on stage holding a long-stemmed red rose. You sniff the rose and you say, 'Ah, the sweet fragrance of my mistress.' Can you do that? Can you remember one lousy line?" "I can do it," says the actor. "Please, give me a chance. I can do it."

"All right," says the producer. "Get down to the theater."

The actor heads down to the theater district. As he's being fitted for the costume, he rehearses the line. Over and over he says it. The first act of the play begins. The actor rehearses backstage. The first act ends; the audience goes out for intermission. The actor rehearses. Intermission ends; the audience returns.

The curtain opens for the second act. The actor walks out and delivers the line – pandemonium ensues. The audience is laughing so hard that the play can't continue. The curtain is lowered. The producer storms out on stage, furious at the actor. "You stupid son-of-a-bitch," he screams, "you ruined my play."

"How?" says the actor. "Did I forget the line?"

"No, you forgot the rose!"

[During the part of the joke when the producer is telling the actor the line he has to memorize, I mime holding a rose. I pretend I am holding it in my right hand, with the stem gripped between my thumb and my first and second fingers. I imagine that the rose is about a foot long, and I hold my right hand about that distance from my face. (You absolutely don't want to get your fingers too close to your nose, otherwise you will telegraph the punch line. Make sure that in your delivery you are emphasizing the memorization; if you place too much importance on the rose you will risk blowing the joke.]

I told this joke to Jay the first day of the convention. He hadn't heard it before, and was delighted with it. I had responsibilities at the theater in the afternoon (I was the music director for the convention) so I couldn't give Jay a ride to the theater, but I did meet up with him after the show and we drove back to the hotel together.

"You know that joke you told me this morning?" he said. "Sure," I said. "Did you get some good reactions with it?"

"No," said Jay. "I couldn't remember the line."

The finale to Jay's act was a ventriloquial routine called "Lefty." Classic in its simplicity, remarkable in its depth of emotion, and devastatingly funny, the routine centered on Jay's attempts to get his cohort Lefty (a rabbit puppet formed from a white glove) to sing *If I Had My Way* (a tune that was made famous by the Mills Brothers in 1931). For twenty-five years (starting in 1980) I had the privilege and pleasure of accompanying Jay on the piano as he performed this bit. The routine was a favorite among magicians, and usually received a standing ovation.

I was happy to play for Jay, and I tried to attend any convention where he would be performing so he wouldn't have to worry about his accompanist. As Jay got older, his memory would occasionally fail him, and, even though he had done the routine thousands of times, he would forget the order of certain bits of business. I tried to make sure that these small slip-ups were unnoticeable to the audience. In *The Linking Ring* (the monthly journal of the I.B.M.), Phil Willmarth wrote of one of these rather jumbled performances, "Jay Marshall was accompanied by Michael Close, who knows the routine backwards and forwards, which is good, because that's the way Jay performs it these days."

Jay was a big part of my life. By a fortunate coincidence he was in Las Vegas when Lisa and I got married, and he was able to attend the festivities. Although it was a much sadder coincidence, Lisa and I happened to be in Chicago when Jay went into the hospital for the final time, and we were able to have one last visit. Jay's memorial service was, as you might expect, a funny affair. On his casket was a sign that read, "Not the first time I died."

I have a treasured memento from Jay. We were together at a small convention a few years before he died. One of the convention organizers had found a commercial birthday card that had a photograph of Jay on it. The photo had been taken in the late 1940s. A young, very dapper Jay Marshall in black tie and tails stood behind a table piled high with magic paraphernalia. Inside, the card said, "Poof! You're old. Happy Birthday." Jay autographed the card for the attendees. I was immensely flattered and honored when the man who, for more than fifty years, had performed in every major venue for audiences all over the world signed my card this way, "To my old friend Mike Close – the finest accompanist I ever had, who has saved my ass on many occasions. With thanks from your pal, Jay Marshall."

He was one of a kind.

Eric

There is a classic Monty Python sketch about a joke that is so funny that it's fatal. The British Army uses it as a secret weapon against the Germans in World War II. The men who translate the joke from English to German are only allowed to see a portion of the joke to protect them from the joke's lethal effectiveness. While you might think that a deadly joke only exists in the world of British sketch comedy, I can assure you that it is possible for a joke to do physical harm. I've seen it happen twice; it's not a pretty sight. (Actually, that's a lie. It's pretty damn hilarious when it happens.)

The following joke seems relatively benign.

> A man walks into a bar. He seems a little hung over. The bartender starts to draw him a beer. "Just a Coke for me, please," says the man. "I really overdid it last night." "That's okay," says the bartender. "Everybody parties a little too hard every now and then."
>
> "No, you don't understand," says the man. "I was drunk out of my mind. When I got home I blew chunks." "It's okay," says the bartender. "Occasionally, we all get sick."
>
> "No, you really don't understand," says the man. "Chunks is my dog."

This joke almost killed Jerry Camaro. Actually, it was merely a mention of the punch line that had such a potent effect. Jerry Camaro was a burly, barrel-chested man who looked like he could be a biker. In fact, Jerry had been a biker. In his younger years, Jerry had been a really bad guy, but he turned his life around, and when I knew him he was a nice guy who smiled and laughed a lot, and who did good close-up magic.

Jerry and I were at a magic convention in Sacramento, California. Along with several hundred other magicians, we were about to watch a lecture by Eric Mead. Eric started his talk with a very funny bit. "The problem with these conventions," he said, "is that you see too much magic. You just can't remember everything you see. I made notes about what I saw at the convention last year, but I can't understand what I've written down." He flipped through a small notebook. "Does this mean anything to anybody? 'Control card with Tamariz Perpendicular Control, run five cards, do Carlyle slough-off, produce card by Forten move.' Anybody?" He flipped a few more pages. "How about this? 'Borrow two rings, do Sephalaljia move with one, load other via Kane card box?' Nobody, huh?" He flipped a few more pages. "How about this, 'Chunks is my dog.'"

Two people in the room knew this joke – Jerry Camaro and me. I thought the reference was funny; Jerry thought it was hilarious. That nobody else knew the joke also struck Jerry as funny. And the fact that the room was absolutely quiet pushed Jerry over the edge. He started to laugh; he tried to hold it in, but he couldn't. He laughed harder. He got up and left the room. I followed him because his face was turning beet red. In the hallway he was laughing and choking and gasping for breath. I got him a glass of water. Jerry finally calmed down enough that we could walk back into the lecture room. It was a scary situation (but, as I mentioned above, also hilarious).

Eric Mead is a young man who lives in Colorado. Eric is an exceptional magician, who performed for many years at the Tower Bar in Aspen. If you have seen the movie *The Aristocrats*, you've seen Eric. He's the guy who does a card trick version of the joke. Eric is one of those people who always seems happy. Every time I see Eric or speak with him on the phone he is cheerful and upbeat. I think the reason for this is that Eric has actually seen the Big Joke, knows what the Ultimate Punch Line is, has decided that it's a shaggy dog story, and realizes that the best way to get through it is to laugh at all the things that happen along the way. Either that or he just does it to piss me off.

Eric has as quick a comedic mind as anyone I've met. When he works, he likes to dance on the edge. One evening some years ago, I was watching him perform at the Tower Bar. One of the women at the bar was an absolutely miserable spectator. She was challenging, obnoxious, uncooperative, unpleasant, and completely unwilling to get into the spirit of fun that Eric was working so hard to establish. Eric handled her with charm and tact, but finally, enough was enough. He put away his cards and said to the woman, "What does your husband do for a living?" She replied, "I'm not married." As Eric turned away to move to another group of people he said, "Well, *there's* a fucking mystery."

Whenever I think of Eric, and I do so often, I am reminded of all the great jokes that take place in bars.

- A man walks into a bar one afternoon. He's the only one in the place. He sits down at the bar and orders a beer. The bartender says to him, "I have to do some work in the stockroom. Is it okay if I just leave you alone for a while?" The man says that it's no problem. The bartender goes into the back room.

  The man sits, drinking his beer; suddenly, he hears a small voice, "That's a nice tie you're wearing. It's a good color for you." The man looks around, but the bar is deserted. He takes another sip of his beer, and again hears the voice. "Have you lost weight? You must be working out, because you're looking good." He gets up and looks behind the bar. There's no one there, and there's no one else in the bar. Shaken, he sits down on the bar stool.

  Just then, the bartender comes back in. "Hey," says the guy, "is there anyone else in the bar besides me?" "No," says the bartender, "why do you ask?"

  "I've been hearing a little voice," says the man. "First it told me that it liked the tie I was wearing, and then it said that I looked like I had lost weight."

  "Oh," says the bartender, "the peanuts are complimentary."

  *

  A man runs into a bar and orders ten shots of whiskey. The bartender lines up the shots, and the man downs them in a rush, one right after the other. The bartender says, "Wow, you drank those in a big hurry."

The man says, "You'd drink fast, too, if you had what I have." The bartender asks, "What do you have?"

The man says, "Seventy-five cents."

*

A man walks into a bar at nine in the morning. He orders a mug of beer. He drinks it and orders another. The man orders beer after beer; he drinks them, never leaving his barstool. At 4:30, the man gets off the barstool, steps away from the bar, unzips his fly, and takes out his member.

"Hey, hey, hey," says the bartender. "You can't piss here."

"I'm not," says the man. "I'm going to piss *way* over there."

*

A Texan walks into a bar. He's drunk, he's mean, and he's looking for a fight. He surveys the bar and says, "Everybody on the right-hand side of the bar is a goddamn son of a polecat." Nobody moves. "All right, then," he says, "everybody on the left-hand side of the bar is a damn queer." One guy slowly steps away from the bar and starts to move.

"Good," says the Texan. "You want to fight?"

"Oh, no," says the man, "I'm on the wrong side."

*

A horse walks into a bar. The bartender says, "Hey, why the long face?"

*

A grasshopper walks into a bar. The bartender says, "Wow, funny you should come in here. We have a drink named after you."

The grasshopper says, "You have a drink called Stanley?"

*

A priest, a rabbi, a hooker, and a kangaroo walk into a bar. The bartender says, "What is this, a joke?"

*

René Descartes walks into a bar. "Would you like something to drink?" asks the bartender. "I think not," replies Descartes, and disappears.

[Google it; you'll laugh and laugh.]

*

A wine expert from the Napa Valley is in a bar in Chicago. He's giving a demonstration of the sensitivity of his pallet. The bartender brings out bottles of wine. The man, who is blindfolded, takes a sip of the wine and identifies the vintner and the year the wine was produced. The man appears to be infallible.

A drunk is watching the proceedings. He pees in a glass and hands it to the man. The man takes a sip and immediately spits it out. "That's piss!" he says. "That's right," says the drunk. "How old am I?"

*

A drunk is sitting at the end of a bar. He says to the bartender, "Let me have another beer, and get that old douche bag at the other end of the bar whatever she wants."

The bartender says to the drunk, "You'll need to watch

your language, sir. This is a respectable place." "Yeah, yeah," says the drunk. "Just bring me my beer and get that old douche bag whatever she wants."

Feeling that the best way to handle the situation is to ignore it, the bartender gives the drunk a beer. He walks to the end of the bar and speaks to the woman sitting there. "I apologize for the man at the other end of the bar. What can I get you to drink?"

She says, "Vinegar and water."

*

A man is sitting at a bar. A beautiful woman walks in and sits down next to him. He buys the woman a drink. "What's your name?" he asks. "My name is Carmen," she says, "and that's the perfect name for me, because I love cars and I love men. What's your name?"

"Beerfuck."

I mentioned in a previous chapter that I always included some jokes in my stand-up show when I worked at Illusions, the restaurant in Carmel, Indiana. Since the shows were done in the bar, it seemed natural to include some bar jokes. The following jokes are the ones I told all the time, and I always told them as if they had happened to me. The first three are visual jokes, but they are among the best visual jokes I've ever told.

A man walked into the bar last night about nine o'clock. He was missing his left hand. [Pull down your left jacket sleeve so it covers your left hand.] The bartender said to him, "Where'd you get that?" The man said, "I lost my hand in Vietnam." The bartender said, "Hey, all disabled veterans get free drinks," and he gave him a beer.

About an hour later, another guy walked in. He looked like this. [Pull down your right jacket sleeve so it covers your right hand.] The bartender said, "Where'd you get that?" The guy said, "I lost my hand in the first Gulf War." The bartender said, "All disabled veterans get free drinks," and he gave him a beer.

Around midnight, another guy walked in. He looked like this. [Adjust your jacket so the sleeves cover both hands.] The bartender said, "Wow, where did you get that?" The man said, "Sears."

[This is one of the great visual jokes of all time. When I told it in England, I used Marks & Spencer as the store, and it worked just fine. At the end of the joke, when you say, "Sears," it's important to lift both arms slightly (still keeping your hands hidden in the sleeves) as if admiring your coat.]

*

I was sitting at the bar last night when a fellow walked in and sat down next to me. This guy had the worst facial tic I'd ever seen. [I start to twitch my right eye, in a winking action.] He ordered a double scotch. I was very curious, so I said to him, "Hey, pal, that's a nasty twitch you've got there."

"It's just a muscle spasm," he replied. "I get it when I'm stressed. I had a really tough day at the office. A couple of aspirin will take care of it." So saying, the guy reached into a pocket and brought out a box of condoms, which he put on the bar. He reached in another pocket and brought out another box of condoms. This guy pulls out eight boxes of condoms before he finally finds his aspirin tin. He takes two aspirin, and a few minutes later the twitch stops. [I stop the twitching action.]

But I've just got to know, so I said, "You know, you're packing a lot of condoms there, pal."

He said, "Hey, have you ever walked into a drugstore and said to the pharmacist, 'I need some aspirin [wink].'" [Pause, then wink again, and again if necessary.]

[Obviously, when you tell the joke, the wink and the twitch look the same. Once I start the twitching action, I continue it as I mime the actions of the man taking out the boxes of condoms.]

*

Last night, a guy came into the bar carrying a small Cairn terrier (like Toto in *The Wizard of Oz*). He put the dog on the bar and said to the bartender and me, "This is a trained dog. Is it worth a beer to see him do his trick?" It was a slow night, so we figured, why not? The bartender gave the guy a beer, and the guy put a Bible on the bar.

"Name a book of the Bible, chapter and verse," he said. I said, "John 3:16." The little dog opened the Bible, flipped through the pages, stopped at one page, and slapped down his little paw. It was on John 3:16. "Is it worth another beer to see him do it again?" the man asked. We said sure, and gave the guy another beer.

I said, "Let's try Exodus 2:9." The dog flipped back through the Bible, stopped on a page, and slapped down his paw. It was on Exodus 2:9.

"The dog is pretty well trained," I said. "Can he heel?" The dog went: [Assume the classic faith healer position – arms extended in front of you, palms of the hands outward, with the right hand slightly above the left hand.]

*

We had an interesting thing happen in the bar last night. One of the patrons got really drunk. He'd been sitting at the bar for quite a while, and when he got off the barstool he fell right on the floor. I ran over and put him back on the stool, but a few minutes later he got off and collapsed again.

I figured that there was no way that this guy could get home by himself, so we called a cab. I got his name and address from his wallet. I tried to walk him out to the cab, but on the way he fell down twice more. I got him in the cab and rode with him to his house. As we walked up his front sidewalk he fell down again, and he fell over twice after I rang the doorbell.

His wife answered the door. I said to her, "Mrs. Jones, I brought your husband home."

She said, "Where's his wheelchair?"

*

I was out walking my Chihuahua Pablo one afternoon. It was really hot. I ran into a buddy of mine who was walking his Golden Retriever. We were in front of one of those 24/7 bars that are everywhere in Las Vegas. My buddy said, "Let's go inside for a drink." I said, "They won't let us in with the dogs." "Sure they will," my buddy said. "Watch what I do."

My buddy put on his sunglasses, walked into the bar, and fumbled his way onto a bar stool. "Give me a beer," he told the bartender. "You can't be in here with the dog," the bartender said. "I'm blind," my friend said. "He's my seeing-eye dog." "Oh, I'm really sorry," said the bartender. "Here's a beer on the house."

I was watching all this through a crack in the door. I put on my sunglasses; Pablo and I marched into the bar, and I fumbled my way onto a bar stool. "Give me a beer," I told the bartender. "You can't be in here with the dog," the bartender said. "I'm blind," I said. "He's my seeing-eye dog."

"Your seeing-eye dog is a Chihuahua?" asked the bartender.

I said, "They gave me a *Chihuahua*?"

That last joke reminds me of this one.

A mousy little man walks into a bar. "Does anyone in here own the German Shepard that's tied up outside?" he asks. "Yeah," says a big biker sitting at the bar. "That's my dog." "Well, I'm sorry to tell you that my dog just killed your dog," the little man says.

The biker gets up off his barstool. "What are you talking about, man? My dog is a trained attack dog. What kind of dog do you have?" "A Chihuahua," replies the little man.

"How could your dog kill my dog?" asks the biker.

"He choked on him."

In addition to the jokes that have a bar as their setting, I also used to tell a series of jokes about what had gone on in the world on that particular day. Here are the four I told most often.

> There was some sad news in the music world today. The man who wrote *The Hokey Pokey* died. It took six hours to get him in his coffin.

*

> I also saw on TV today that J.L. Heinz III, the grandson of the man who founded the Heinz "57 Varieties" Food Corporation died. He was an old man, and his last request was to have his ashes scattered over Lake Erie. Apparently, he had grown up in a little town on the lake. Anyway, there was some very touching footage on CNN this morning of his family on a boat on the lake with his ashes, going: [make your left hand into a fist and pound it with the palm of your right hand as if pounding the bottom of a ketchup bottle.]

*

> Mike Tyson is in trouble again. He was hit with an assault charge in Las Vegas. Apparently, he was at a Pizza Hut with Don King and a lawyer. A little old lady was waiting on them. At the end of the meal, she saw that about a third of the pizza hadn't been eaten, so she said to Tyson, "Do you wanna box for the pizza?" [Wait for the laugh; it may take a moment.] She landed a few punches, but it was a "reach" thing...

*

> The biggest story in the news today took place at O'Hare Airport. There was a flight from Chicago to Dallas. The passengers were boarding from the middle of the plane, and when the pilot and co-pilot came on board, they appeared to be blind. The pilot had dark glasses and a cane, and the co-pilot had a seeing-eye

dog. They fumbled their way to the cockpit and closed the door. There was some nervous laughter among the passengers, but they shrugged it off. A few minutes later, the plane pushed back and taxied to the runway.

The plane began to take off. It charged down the runway, going faster and faster. But the plane stayed on the ground. There it was, going hell-bent for leather, down the runway, on the ground. One of the passengers, a woman, pressed her face against the window. She could see the end of the runway and the Interstate highway beyond it. She let out a scream. This freaked out all the other passengers, and they all started screaming. Just then, the plane lifted off and headed into the sky.

When the plane reached cruising altitude, the co-pilot turned to the pilot and said, "You know, one of these days they're not going to scream."

The Mike Tyson joke above reminded me of this one.

The year is 1992 and Mike Tyson goes to prison for his rape conviction. On his first day of incarceration, he is sitting dejectedly in his cell. His cellmate says to him, "I know you're feeling bad now, but life in prison is okay. For example, on Mondays we get to use the library. They have lots of books and current magazines. There's even a law library so you can work on your appeal. You like to read?" Tyson says, "No."

"Well," says the cellmate, "you're not gonna like Mondays. But on Tuesdays we do arts and crafts. You can draw in pastels or charcoal, or paint in watercolors. Maybe do a sculpture in clay. You like arts and crafts?" "No," says Tyson.

"Well, you're not gonna like Tuesdays. Are you gay?" asks the cellmate. "No!" says Tyson.

"You gonna *hate* Wednesdays."

The first time I ever made money doing magic, I was seventeen years old. I was hired to do magic in the bar in the Moose Lodge in Lebanon, Indiana. When I opened the side door that led to the bar, the smoke rolled out like a London fog. There were only a few people in the bar. Some men were playing cards; others sat a table, talking quietly. The only likely prospect was a man sitting at the bar, staring at his drink. I was scared to death, but I decided it was safest to start with him.

I took out my cards and began to shuffle them. "Hi, I'm Michael, and I'm doing magic here this evening. Let me show you a quick trick. Please, take a card." I fanned the cards and offered the fan to the man. He looked at me blearily, but didn't move. "It's okay, this is a really good trick, and it only takes a moment. I wouldn't waste your time. Please, pull out a card." Again, the man looked at me but did nothing.

I figured that the most expedient solution was to select a card for him. I pulled a card out of the fan and showed it to him. "This is your card," I said to him.

He looked up at me and said, "Atsa fuckin' miracle," and passed out.

My friend, magician/comedian Doc Dixon, says that everything is funnier with monkeys. So, let's end this chapter with a monkey in a bar joke.

> A man walks into a bar with a monkey on his shoulder. He sits down at the bar and orders a beer. The bartender says, "You can't be in here with the monkey." The man says, "He's a trained monkey. He's very well behaved. He won't be a problem."
>
> The bartender serves the man a beer, and while he's drinking it, the monkey jumps off his shoulder, runs to the pool table, and swallows the cue ball. The bartender is furious. "Get that monkey the hell out of my bar," he shouts. The man gathers up the monkey, and they both leave.
>
> Two days later, the man returns to the bar. He is holding the cue ball; the monkey is on his shoulder. He places the ball on the pool table and sits down at the bar. "I don't want that monkey in my bar," says the bartender. "I promise you, he'll behave himself. Let me have a beer, please," says the man.

As the man drinks his beer, the monkey jumps off his shoulder and picks out a peanut from a bowl on the bar. He sticks the peanut up his rear end, takes it out, and eats it. He picks out another peanut, sticks it up his rear end, takes it out, and eats it.

"What the hell is that all about?" asks the bartender. "Well," says the man, "ever since the cue ball incident he checks for size first."

Aldo

I mentioned in the previous chapter that I was present on two occasions when the telling of a joke produced near fatal results. Eric Mead was responsible for the first one; I was responsible for the second. It happened when I told what I thought was a fairly innocuous joke to my friend Aldo Colombini. I should tell you that Aldo is not the same Aldo Colombini as Kowalski, the Polish guy who changed his name in a joke in an earlier chapter. I just used Aldo's name in the joke because the only other Italian name I could think of was Benito Mussolini, and that wouldn't have been funny.

Aldo is from Bologna, Italy, and came to the United States in 1993. In a short time, he has managed to accomplish something very difficult – he has learned to be funny in a second language. Comedy is not just about words; it is also about the rhythm of a language, the speed of delivery, the cultural references and sensibilities, and the pacing of a punch line. This varies from country to country. I remember performing at a convention in Sweden. The Swedes have excellent English language skills, and I was able to do some jokes that were well received. But on the gala evening show, the emcee, who was Swedish, absolutely killed. I couldn't understand a word he said, but I did notice that the rhythm of his delivery was different than that I associate with American comedians. Man, I thought, how great would it be as an American, to get laughs like that in Swedish.

Aldo has not only improved his vocabulary skills to the point where he can deliver (and understand) American jokes, he has also absorbed the rhythm of American humor. He favors short, direct jokes ("Summertime was bad for me; my parents made me stay with my grandparents. I hate the cemetery."), and he gets big, genuine laughs from his audiences.

In 1996 the I.B.M convention was held in Oakland, California. Aldo and I were hanging out at the bar after one of the evening shows. I told Aldo this joke.

> The location is a home in Tampa, Florida. It is New Year's Day. A man is sitting on his couch; he hears a knock at his front door. He opens the door. There is no one there, but a snail is sitting on the front porch. The man kicks the snail off the porch and into the front yard.
>
> On Thanksgiving Day of that year, the man hears a knock on his front door. He opens the door; the snail is sitting on the front porch. The snail says, "What the fuck was that all about?"

Admittedly, this is a silly joke, but it's a good one. For Aldo, it was the funniest joke he had ever heard while standing at a bar in Oakland, California. He started to laugh, and the more he laughed the funnier the joke became. He eventually reached the point where, just like Jerry Camaro, he couldn't catch his breath. His face turned red and he gasped for air. I thought we were going to lose him. Finally, he calmed down enough to get his wind back.

Thinking of Aldo brings back many memories, and a wide variety of jokes comes to mind. First, of course, are the Italian jokes.

> A magician gets a gig in Italy. At JFK airport, he boards a flight to Rome. As he is getting comfortable in his seat, a flight attendant walks by. "Bon giorno," she says to the magician. "Huh?" he replies. "You don't speak any Italian?" she asks. "Not a word," the magician replies. "How long will you be in Italy?" she asks. "About six months," the magician says.
>
> "Well, listen," says the flight attendant. "When we get airborne, put on your headphones and tune to channel 11. You can hear basic Italian lessons there. We have an eight-hour flight ahead of us. By the time we reach Rome you'll have learned enough Italian to get around the city." "Thanks," says the magician.
>
> The flight takes off, and for eight hours the magician listens to the Italian lessons. The plane lands in Rome;

the magician deplanes and heads toward the immigration area. The immigration agent says, "Buena sera." The magician says, "Kkckkckkkskzzkzk." [This is the sound of electric static.]

[This is a great joke to tell on stage, and I have often done so. Using a microphone enhances the static noise at the end of the joke.]

*

Classified ad: For sale - World War II Italian rifle. Never fired; only dropped once.

The premise of learning to speak Italian reminds me of a joke Penn Jillette told me. It's a Newfie joke (Penn's family comes from Newfoundland).

A Newfoundlander is going to visit Italy. He is worried because he doesn't speak the language. A friend says to him, "You have nothing to worry about. If you want to be understood, JUST...SPEAK...SLOWLY...AND...LOUDLY. YOU'LL...BE...FINE."

The Newfoundlander flies to Rome. His first evening there, he walks into a bar. "I...WOULD...LIKE...A... BEER...PLEASE," he says. The bartender looks at him quizzically. "ARE...YOU...FROM...NEWFOUNDLAND?" he asks.

"Yes." "ARE...YOU...FROM...NEWFOUNDLAND?" he asks the bartender.

"Yes," says the bartender.

"WAIT...A...MINUTE" says the Newfoundlander. "IF... YOU...ARE...FROM...NEWFOUNDLAND...AND...I'M... FROM...NEWFOUNDLAND...WHY...ARE...WE...SPEAKING... ITALIAN?"

*

A crowd has gathered in St. Peter's Square in the Vatican to receive the Sunday morning blessing from the

Pope. Instead of the Pope, however, a Bishop walks out onto the balcony. Some murmuring and muttering rises up from the crowd.

The Bishop holds up his hands to silence the crowd, and says, "Listen up; I got some real bad news. The Pope, he's real sick." "Oh, no," says the crowd, "God save the Pope." "The Pope, he's gonna need a heart transplant." "Oh, no," says the crowd as one. "Take *my* heart; take *my* heart."

The Bishop is overwhelmed with emotion. "Oh," he says, "you are such good people. But we gotta be fair. I'm gonna throw this feather into the crowd. Whoever the feather land on, you gonna give your heart to save the Pope." "Take my heart; take my heart," chants the crowd.

"What good people you are," says the Bishop, fighting back tears. He throws the feather off the balcony. As the feather floats into the crowd you can see people saying, "Take my heart. Phewt. [Turn your head and blow away an imaginary feather.] Take my heart. Phewt."

[This is another joke that plays great for a large audience. I confess that when I tell this joke, I do a very stereotypical Italian accent, saying "take-a my heart" and "you are such-a good people." I implied that in the write up, but thought I should make it clear.]

*

During the Dark Ages, the Pope decreed that all the Jews had to leave Rome. The Jewish community was understandably upset. The Pope offered to have a religious debate with any member of the Jewish community. If the Jewish representative won the debate, the Jews could stay in Rome.

None of the Rabbis wanted the responsibility of debating the Pope. Finally, Moishe, the janitor of the Temple, said that he would do the debate. Moishe, however, spoke no Italian, and the Pope spoke no Hebrew, so it was decided that they would debate silently.

The day of the great debate arrived. The Pope and Moishe sat on opposite sides of a table in St. Peter's Square. Hundreds of interested onlookers surrounded them. The Pope began by holding up three fingers. Moishe replied by holding up one finger. The Pope was taken aback by this. He hesitated, and then waved a single finger in circles over his head. Moishe responded by pointing to the ground. Again, the Pope was surprised by Moishe's response. He thought for several minutes, and then brought out a communion wafer and a chalice of wine. Moishe placed an apple on the table.

"Enough," said the Pope. "I concede. This man has bested me in the debate. The Jews can stay in Rome." The Pope returned to his office, where he was surrounded by Cardinals, all wanting to know what happened. "He had an answer for everything," said the Pope. "I held up three fingers, representing the Holy Trinity. He held up one finger, reminding me that, though we were of two different religions, we shared the same God. Then I waved my finger around me to represent that God was all around us. He pointed to the ground to show that God was right here, right now. Then I brought out the wine and the wafer to show that God absolves us of our sins. He brought out an apple to remind me that we are all born into original sin. He was too clever. What could I do?"

When Moishe returned to the Temple, the Rabbis crowded around him, eager to know what had happened. "Well," said Moishe, "the Pope said he wanted all the Jews out of Rome in three days. I said 'Up yours.' He said all the Jews would be rounded up and cleared out. I said the Jews are staying right here." "Then what happened?" asked a Rabbi.

"Nothing. We broke for lunch."

For some reason, that joke reminded me of this one.

A journalist is spending a week in Jerusalem. Her hotel room window overlooks the Wailing Wall. Her first morning there, she looks out her window and sees an old Jewish man walking toward the wall. He is there for an hour and then he slowly walks away. Later that

> afternoon, she sees the same man walking to the wall. He stays for an hour, and then slowly leaves.
>
> This scenario happens every day for a week. On the morning of her last day in Jerusalem, she sees the old man walking toward the wall. She runs downstairs and stops the man in the street. "I'm sorry to bother you," she says, "but I've watched you every day this week. Do you always come to the wall twice a day?" "Yes," says the old man, "I have been doing this for thirty years."
>
> "Can you tell me about this ritual?" she asks. "In the morning," says the old man, "I come to the wall and I pray for the eradication of disease and an end to world hunger. Then I go home and I eat a little lunch. In the afternoon, I walk back and I pray for world peace, especially peace between the Israelis and the Palestinians."
>
> "And you have been doing this for thirty years?" asks the reporter. "Yes," says the man. "How does that make you feel?" she asks.
>
> "Like I've been talking to a fucking wall."

Thoughts of the snail joke that hurt Aldo bring to mind some great animal jokes.

> A jockey gets a phone call from a distraught race horse owner. The owner's jockey has fallen in the shower and has a broken arm. The owner needs a jockey for a race that afternoon. The jockey gets to the race grounds and meets with the owner. "This race is in the form of a steeplechase," says the owner. "Here's what you need to do. Just before you come to a barricade, you need to lean down to the horse's ear and say, 'One, two, three, jump. One, two, three, jump.' Have you got it?" The jockey says, "Sure," but thinks to himself, "Yeah, tell me how to do my job."
>
> The race starts. When the horse nears the first jump, the jockey says nothing. The horse runs right into the barricade, and the jockey is badly shaken. The horse is two lengths behind the pack. At the second hurdle, which is a hedge, the jockey says nothing. The horse

plows into the hedge, and the jockey is nearly knocked off. The horse is now six lengths behind.

At the third hurdle, the jockey leans forward and whispers, "One, two, three, jump." The horse leaps like Pegasus. He clears the hurdle easily and begins to pick up speed. At every barrier the jockey whispers, "One, two, three, jump," and the horse jumps it with ease. The horse runs like the wind, and wins the race by a nose.

At the winner's circle, the jockey dismounts and the owner comes up to him. "I watched how you handled that race," he tells the jockey. "You didn't say, 'One, two, three, jump' at the first two hurdles, did you." "Of course I did," says the jockey, trying to cover his butt. "I just think your horse is deaf."

"No, he's not *deaf*," says the owner, "he's *blind*."

*

A matronly woman is visiting the San Diego Zoo. She is standing in front of the porcupine exhibit. She studies the animals for a moment and then calls over a zoo keeper. "Excuse me, young man," she says. "What is the difference between an African porcupine and a North American porcupine?" "The main difference," says the zoo keeper, "is that the African porcupine's pricks are longer."

The woman is outraged at the rudeness of the zoo keeper. She drags him to the office of the director of the zoo, and she reads the riot act to both of them. When she finishes, the zoo director says, "Madam, I sincerely apologize for my employee. What occurred here was a simple mix up of terminology. What he meant to say was that the African porcupine's 'quills' are longer. Their pricks are about the same size."

*

A man is walking down the street when he sees an unusual sight. A hearse is driving slowly down the street. Behind the hearse, a man is walking a Chihuahua.

Behind him is a long line of men, walking single file. Overcome with curiosity, the first man walks up to the man with the dog. "What's going on here?" he asks.

"My wife and my mother-in-law are in the hearse. We're on our way to the cemetery." "What happened?" asks the first man. "Well, my little dog here bit them, and they both died."

"My goodness," says the first man, and then he thinks for a minute. "Say," he says, "could I borrow that dog?"

"Get in line."

*

A woman wakes up one morning to hear a terrible ruckus up on her roof. She walks outside and sees a full grown gorilla jumping around on her roof. She calls animal control, explains the situation, and they promise to send someone right over.

A few minutes later, the animal control truck drives up. A man gets out. He sets a ladder against the house. Then he opens the back of the truck, and takes out a Chihuahua, which he places on the ground by the ladder. He then removes a broom from the truck and he straps on a gun.

The man climbs the ladder; he has the broom in one hand. He approaches the gorilla and begins to poke at him with the broom. The gorilla swings back. The man pokes again. The gorilla makes a big swing, and goes slightly off balance. The man hits the gorilla in the butt with the broom, and the gorilla rolls off the roof and hits the ground. The instant he hits, the Chihuahua runs over, grabs the gorilla by the balls, drags him over to the truck, and tosses him into the back. By this time the man has come down the ladder, and he slams the back door closed.

The woman is quite impressed by this exhibition. She says to the man, "That was really something. But I was wondering, why do you wear a gun?"

"Well," says the man, "every now and then a gorilla

will knock me off the roof, and I've got to shoot that dog."

*

A blind man and his seeing-eye dog are approaching a busy intersection. The light turns red, but the dog heads out into the street anyway, taking his owner with him. Cars hit their brakes, swerve wildly, and honk their horns as the man and the dog scramble their way across the street. When the man reaches the opposite side, he fumbles in his pocket, eventually bringing out a dog biscuit.

Another man has been watching all this. He says to the blind man, "That dog almost got you killed. You're going to reward him?"

"No," says the blind man. "I'm just trying to find his head so I can kick him in the ass."

*

A blind man is learning to sky dive. He has received all his ground training and is about to make his first solo jump. Some of his friends are very concerned.

"Are you sure you'll be all right up there?" asks one.

"I'll be fine," the blind man says. "When we get ready to jump, I'll put my hand on the shoulder of the person ahead of me, so I know when we reach the door. I'll feel it when he jumps out, and I'll move until I feel the edge of the door. When the drill instructor says to go, I'll jump out. I'll turn my body so the wind hits me in the face. I'll count ten seconds and then I'll pull the rip cord. If I don't immediately feel my body being jerked up, I'll know that something is wrong, and I'll pull the emergency chute."

"But when you're about six feet above the ground you need to bend your knees in preparation for impact. How are you going to know when to do that?"

"The leash will go slack."

*

A young polar bear walks up to his mother. He asks, "Mom, am I a real polar bear?" "Yes, son," she replies, "you're a real polar bear."

The young polar bear finds his father. "Dad," he asks, "am I a real polar bear?" "Yes, son, you're a real polar bear."

The young polar bear walks up to his grandfather. "Grandfather, am I a real polar bear?" "Yes, you're a real polar bear. Why do you ask?"

"Because I'm freezing my ass off."

The joke you just read has a special place in my heart. My wife, Lisa, is Canadian. Even though she grew up in Toronto, she has the least tolerance for cold of anyone I've ever met. We are the couple that dual climate control in cars was invented for. For Christmas a few years ago, my sister Janet made her an adult-sized pair of footie pajamas. Embroidered on the pocket was a polar bear with the words "Am I a real polar bear?" underneath. Lisa wears them. And we live in Vegas.

- A man is out duck hunting. He's had a miserable day; he hasn't shot one duck. As he's heading back to his car, a lone duck flies overhead. He fires at it, and the duck falls behind some trees. The man walks to where the duck fell, and sees that it has landed in a farmer's front yard. The farmer is standing over the duck. The hunter walks over and starts to pick up the bird.

  "What do you think you're doing there, young fella?" asks the farmer. "I'm retrieving my duck," says the hunter. "I'm afraid you're mistaken," says the farmer, "that's my duck." "No, you're mistaken," says the hunter. "I just shot that duck, and I'm taking it with me."

  "Well, in these parts," says the farmer, "whatever is on your land is yours. And since that duck is on my land, it belongs to me. But since we have a dispute here, I think we should settle it the way we settle things in these parts. Since I am the disputed party, I will kick you in the groin as I hard as I can. Then, you can kick me in the groin as hard as you can. And we'll go back and forth until someone relinquishes his claim on the duck. I go first."

With that, the farmer pulls back and kicks the hunter in the groin. Searing pain drops the hunter to the ground. He rolls around for ten minutes, unable to draw a breath deep enough to make a sound. Then, he screams and rolls for ten minutes. After five more minutes he is able to catch his breath, and stands up.

"Okay, okay," he says to the farmer. "Now it's my turn."

The farmer says, "Naw, take the duck."

That reminds me.

Two guys go hunting. As they are walking through the woods, one of them suddenly grimaces, grabs his chest, and falls to the ground. The other hunter is completely freaked out. He takes out his cell phone and dials 911. When the operator answers he says, "I need help. I'm out here in the woods and my friend has had a heart attack. I think he's dead."

"Calm down, calm down," says the operator. "I'm here to help you. First, make sure that he's really dead." The operator hears silence, then…BANG, then the hunter says, "Okay, now what?"

*

Two guys go hunting. They get separated. The first guy hears a noise. He turns and fires, and shoots his buddy in the chest. He carries his friend back to the car and drives him to the hospital. He carries him into the emergency room. He says to the attending doctor, "Will he be all right?"

The doctor says, "He would have been, if you hadn't gutted him."

Aldo's language skills remind me of a rare category of jokes – jokes about language. Here are two of the best.

The American Society of Semanticists is holding their annual convention. The keynote speaker is a professor from Rutgers who is presenting the results of a forty-year research program.

"For the past forty years," he says, beginning his speech, "my staff of undergraduates, graduate students, post-graduate students, and research fellows has read every book, newspaper, and magazine published in the United States. They have watched every television show and listened to a carefully selected sampling of radio programs from around the country. We have discovered that in English it is possible for a double negative to have a positive connotation, as in the sentence, 'There isn't a day when I don't think about her.' And it is possible for a double negative to have a negative connotation as in the sentence, 'I ain't got nobody.' But it is never possible for a double *positive* to have a negative connotation."

A guy in the front row says, "Yeah, right."

*

A worldwide conference of linguists is meeting in Basil, Switzerland. They are there to determine, once and for all, which is the most beautiful language. All the linguists are eager to be heard. The Swiss chairman calls on the representative from England.

"English is the language of Shakespeare; the language of great plays, poetry, and sonnets. Could there possibly be a more beautiful word than the English word 'butterfly?'" He sits down and the hands of the other delegates shoot up. The German representative is frantically trying to be recognized, but the chairman calls on the French delegate.

"English may indeed be the language of poetry, but French is the language of love. And in French, the word for butterfly is papillon. Papillon – what a beautiful word." The Frenchman sits down, and the delegates strive for attention. The German is waving his hands wildly, but the chairman calls on the representative from Italy.

"English may be the language of poetry and French the language of love, but Italian is the language of music and opera. And in Italian, the word for butterfly is farfalla. Farfalla – what a beautiful word."

The German representative stands up, pounds his hands on his desk, and shouts, "What is wrong with Schmetterling?"

Finally, here is the best almost-clean animal joke I have ever told. I used it to end my stand-up magic act. I'll get into the joke the way I did when I performed it.

Thanks for laughing at the jokes tonight. If I have any skill as a joke teller, it's due to my grandmother. She loved to tell jokes. She also had an interesting outlook on life. She said to me, "Michael, remember this. No matter how popular you think you are, or how many friends you think you have, attendance at your funeral will depend on the weather." My one great regret in life is that I never found out if she was right. The day they buried her it was raining, and I didn't much feel like going...

Anyway, this is a joke that my grandmother told me. A circus bus is making its way up a very steep winding road. Suddenly, the bus goes out of control and crashes through the guardrail. It plunges down the face of a cliff. The bus is totally destroyed. There are people parts and animal parts scattered on the face of the cliff. It's a horrible accident.

The police and the fire rescue units show up. The chief of police sees a monkey sitting on a rock, apparently the only survivor of this crash. The chief says to the monkey, "You were on the bus?" The monkey goes like this: [shake your head up and down slowly]. The chief asks, "What was happening on the bus?" The monkey goes like this: [Mime drinking a bottle of beer.] "They were drinking on the bus?" The monkey shakes his head yes.

"What else was happening on the bus?" The monkey goes like this: [Mime taking a hit off a joint.] "They were smoking dope on the bus?" The monkey shakes his head yes. "What else was happening?" The monkey goes like this: [Thrust your hips back and forth in a humping gesture.] "They were having sex on the bus?" The monkey shakes his head yes.

"Well, what were you doing?" The monkey goes: [Mime driving a bus while looking over your right shoulder.]

Billy

Billy McComb was of the same generation as Jay Marshall, and he too achieved great success as a performer. He appeared on big stages, variety halls, and workingmen's clubs, and he starred on television in the United Kingdom. Unlike Jay, who retired from active performing to run his magic shop, Billy kept plugging away until just a few months before his death. He was regularly featured at the Magic Castle in Hollywood, and he was often the opening act for The Amazing Johnathan in Las Vegas. Feeling some trepidation, I went to one of Billy's appearances in Vegas. I could not imagine how an audience that had paid money to see Johnathan would react to seeing a frail-looking old man walking out on stage. I needn't have worried. Billy walked out slowly, as if a strong breeze would blow him away. "Don't worry," he told the audience, "I won't be out here long. It's rice pudding night back at the home." He then proceeded to charm and baffle everyone in the theater.

Like Jay, Billy was a walking encyclopedia of magic history. Many of his magical creations are in the acts of today's working professionals. And man, was he funny. My wife Lisa first met him at the Magic Castle. Billy sat down next to her at the bar outside the Palace of Mystery showroom. "Hello, my dear," he said to her, overdoing his English accent. "I understand that you're the one who's going to cure my impotence problem." On another occasion, I sat with Billy at the bar as he tried to explain to me a trick using a cocktail napkin. He blew on the corners of the napkin, trying to separate the four layers. "Sometimes when I do this," he said, "the napkin spontaneously combusts."

Billy was born in Ireland. As a young man, he attended and graduated from medical school in England. Billy had pursued this career in an effort to please his family (his father had been knighted for his research into X-ray technology), but soon discovered that his real calling was in show business. Whenever I think of Billy, I'm reminded of doctor jokes. The following are among my favorites.

> My doctor called me today. "I've got good news and I've got bad news," he said. "I don't want to hear any bad news," I replied. "What's the good news?"
>
> He said, "They're going to name a disease after you."

*

> My doctor called me today. "I've got bad news and I've got worse news," he said. "What's the bad news?" I asked. "You've got twenty-four hours to live."
>
> "What's the worse news?" I asked. "I was supposed to call you yesterday."

*

> My doctor called me today. "We have your test results back," he said. "You have ten..."
>
> "Ten what!" I shouted. "Ten weeks, ten months?"
>
> "Nine...eight...seven...six..."

*

> My doctor called me today. "I have bad news for you. You have AIDS, and you have Alzheimer's." "Well," I said, "at least I don't have AIDS."

*

> My doctor called me today. "We have your test results back," he said. "You're a goner."
>
> "What?" I said. "There has to be something you can do." "Nope," said the doctor. "Oh, come on," I said. With all the advances in medical science, there isn't anything you can do?" "Not that I can think of," said the doctor.

"This is ridiculous," I said. "There must be treatment." "Well," said the doctor, "you might try mud baths."

"Will that help?" I asked. "No," he said, "but it will get you used to dirt."

*

A man with a terrible flatulence problem goes to the doctor. He's admitted to a small examination room, and he sits, waiting for the doctor. A few minutes later, the doctor comes in. "What seems to be the problem?" asks the doctor.

"Well," says the man, "I have a [farting noise] big problem with flatulence [farting noise]. I've tried to change my [farting noise] diet, I've used various [farting noise] off-the-shelf remedies [farting noise], but nothing seems to work [farting noise]. It's getting to the point [farting noise] where it's affecting my personal [farting noise] life."

The doctor says, "Hang on just a minute." He leaves the examination room, and comes back a few minutes later carrying a six-foot long pole with a big brass hook on the end. "Jesus Christ," says the man, "what are you going to do with that?"

The doctor says, "I'm going to open a window!"

[If for some reason it isn't obvious, you make the farting noise with your mouth. If you do it any other way, your audience won't hang around to hear the punch line.]

*

Two men are sitting in a doctor's waiting room. One says to the other, "Wh-wh-wh-why are y-y-y-you h-h-h-h-here?" "I have an enlarged prostate," says the other.

"Wh-wh-wh-wh-wh-what is an enla-la-la-la-la-larged p-p-p-p-p-p-p-prostate?" asks the first.

"I piss like you talk."

[I love telling this joke, and I make the first man's stammer into a big production. If you plan on telling this joke, work on your stammering. It makes or breaks the joke.]

*

A man with a tapeworm goes to a doctor who has been recommended to him. He sits in the examination room. Soon, the doctor comes in. "I have a tapeworm," says the man. "No one has been able to get rid of it. I was told that you have a cure." "You've come to the right place," says the doctor. "I have a guaranteed treatment." The doctor leaves for a moment and returns carrying a shelled hardboiled egg and a lemon cookie.

"Please drop your trousers and bend over the examination table," says the doctor. The man complies, and the doctor shoves the egg up the man's rear end. He then shoves the lemon cookie up the man's butt. "That's all for today," says the doctor. "Come back next week." The man looks puzzled, but he readjusts his clothing and awkwardly leaves the office.

The next week the man returns to the doctor's office and is ushered into an examination room. The doctor enters carrying a shelled hardboiled egg and a lemon cookie. Again, he instructs the man to remove his trousers and bend over the examination table. As before, he shoves the egg and the lemon cookie up the man's rear end. "That's it," the doctor announces. "Come back next week." Again, the man staggers uncomfortably out of the office.

He comes back the next week and awaits the doctor in the examination room. The doctor comes in with the egg and the cookie. "You know, doc," the man says, "this is a very uncomfortable situation. How long does this go on?" "After this treatment, we have three more sessions," says the doctor, "and I guarantee that we will get rid of your tapeworm." The man bends over, and the shelled hardboiled egg and the lemon cookie go up his rear end.

The treatment continues. On his sixth visit, the man waits in the examination room. The doctor enters; he's holding a shelled hardboiled egg and a hammer. "Today's the last session," says the doctor. "Drop your pants and bend over the table." The man does as he's told. The doctor shoves the egg up the man's rear end and stands at the ready with the hammer. Five minutes pass. Suddenly, the tapeworm pokes his head out of the man's ass and says, "Hey, where's my cookie?" And the doctor goes [mime the gesture of smashing the tapeworm with the hammer.]

*

An old man goes to the doctor. He says to him, "I can't piss." The doctor asks, "How old are you?" "I'm ninety-three," says the old man. The doctor says, "You've pissed enough."

*

A doctor is examining an old man. The man, a retired army colonel, is in excellent shape. His eyes are sharp, he has a full head of steel-gray hair, and he's trim and extremely fit. The doctor is impressed. "Tell me," he asks the man, "when is the last time you had sex?" "Nineteen forty-five," replies the man. "And you can remember that?" asks the doctor. "Of course," says the man, "it's only 21:30 now."

*

A man arrives at his psychiatrist's office at nine in the morning. He doesn't have an appointment, but he coerces the receptionist into letting him see the doctor. He rushes into the doctor's office and frantically begins his story.

"I'm really sorry to barge in here without an appointment, but the most frightening thing happened to me last night. I dreamt about my mother. I saw her cooking in the kitchen in the house I lived in as a boy. She was wearing a familiar dress with an apron tied around her waist, and her hair was brown, styled the way she wore it when she was young. But when I looked at her, she had *your face*! I woke up in a cold sweat. I took a quick shower, threw on some clothes, had a cup of coffee, and headed right down to your office to see you."

The psychiatrist says, "*Coffee*? You call that *breakfast*?"

*

A man walks into a doctor's office one evening. "You've got to help me," he says. "I think I'm a moth."

"Actually, I'm a general practitioner, not a psychiatrist," says the doctor. "Why did you come to me?"

The man says, "Your light was on."

*

A man visits Hong Kong on a business trip. One evening, he goes out on the town with some clients, parties a little bit too hard, and ends up in a brothel. A few days later he returns to the United States.

He's been back home about a week when he notices a bright red rash on his genitals. He goes to his doctor, who runs a battery of tests. "I have some really bad news," says the doctor. "You have what's known as Hong Kong Dong. There is no known treatment, nor is there any cure. The only thing we can do is surgically remove your genitals." The man is justifiably freaked out. He seeks a second opinion from the best urologist in the city. That doctor comes to the same conclusions – the man has Hong Kong Dong, there is no cure, and the only solution is the surgical removal of his genitals.

The man travels around the country trying to find someone who can help him. He ends up at the Mayo Clinic, but the doctors concur with the opinions of the previous doctors. The man is utterly depressed. Suddenly, he has an inspiration: he caught the disease in Hong Kong; perhaps he can find the cure there.

He flies to Hong Kong and spends several days tracking down the city's foremost expert in herbal medicine. The doctor's office is at the end of a long narrow street. He enters, and sees an old, wizened Chinese man sitting at a cluttered desk. "I've traveled a long way to seek out your help," says the man, and he shows the doctor his rash. "Holy cow," says the doctor, "you've got Hong Kong Dong." "I know," says the man. "I've been to every medical expert in the United States, and they all say that the only way to treat it is the surgical removal of my genitals."

"Ah," says the old man, "American doctors are full of honorable shit. There is absolutely no need for surgical removal of balls and dick." "Really," says the man, "that's wonderful."

"Yeah," says the doctor. "Wait three weeks; they'll fall off by themselves."

*

A man suffers from severe migraine headaches. He has tried everything – all the over-the-counter remedies, prescription drugs, acupuncture, meditation, bio-feedback – nothing alleviates the pain.

The man goes to the Mayo Clinic in Rochester, Minnesota, where he undergoes a battery of tests. After several days of being prodded, probed, stuck, scanned, and scrutinized, the man is visited by the head of medicine of the clinic. "We believe that we can eliminate your headaches," says the doctor. "You have a very rare condition; your testicles press on your spine, and this pressure is causing your headaches. If we remove your testicles, the headaches will go away. Obviously, this is an important, life-changing decision. Give it some thought, and let me know what you want to do."

The man isn't happy with the situation, but sees no way that he can continue living with the constant pain of the headaches. He agrees to the operation. The surgery is successful, and the man leaves the hospital a few days later. Although he is still tender, he is amazed at how good he feels. In fact, he feels better than he has in years. "This is the beginning of a brand new phase of my life," he thinks. He decides to reward himself with a completely new outfit.

He goes to the most exclusive men's clothing store in Rochester. A well-dressed older man greets him. "I'd like a whole new wardrobe," says the man. "Very good," says the clerk, who walks around him, eying him carefully. "I'd say you wear a 42 Regular suit, you take a 32 sleeve and a 16 neck in a shirt, you wear a size-10 shoe, and you wear 36-inch-waist boxer shorts."

The man is very surprised. "That's amazing. You're almost exactly right," he says. "But you got the underwear wrong. I wear 34-inch briefs." "I don't think so," says the clerk. "I'm telling you," says the man, "I've worn 34-inch briefs since high school."

"I'll take your word for it," says the clerk, "but 34-inch briefs would squeeze your testicles and give you terrible headaches."

*

A couple has their first child. Unfortunately, when the baby is born, it's just a head. Remarkably, the head survives, and they name it Jimmy.

On Jimmy's twelfth birthday, the family gets a phone call from a doctor in Los Angeles. "I have some extraordinary news for you," he says. "There was a car accident in L.A. this morning. Tragically, a twelve-year-old boy was decapitated in the crash. We were able to keep his body functioning, and I believe we can transplant your son onto this body. He should be able to live a normal, active life. Get on a plane to L.A. right now, and we'll start the surgery immediately."

The couple is overjoyed. They run into their son's room. "Jimmy," says the mother, "we have the most wonderful surprise for you for your birthday."

Jimmy says, "It's not another fuckin' hat, is it?"

[A version of this joke ends with the punch line "Quit while you're a head." If you start to tell the one above, you'll have to tell your audience not to interrupt you, because it isn't the joke they think it's going to be.]

Billy

Billy McComb was as quick as anyone I've ever known, and he had an uncanny ability to find the joke hidden in any situation. Chuck Fayne (who you will learn more about in the next chapter) knew Billy for more than thirty years. One evening, Chuck was at the Magic Castle when someone ran in saying that an ambulance was taking Billy to the hospital. At the time, Billy lived in an apartment next door to the Castle. Chuck ran outside, saw the ambulance, and hopped in the back with Billy. Billy motioned for Chuck to lean in closer, and said to him, "If this lighting is for the paramedics, that's okay. If it's for me, I'd like a little more pink."

Of course, there are times when having a quick wit can get you into trouble. One time, Billy was visiting Australia. The immigration officer was in a lousy mood, and he was giving Billy a lot of grief. "Do you have a criminal record?" he asked. "Why," replied Billy, "is it still mandatory?" It took a while for Billy to enter the country.

Billy had some great self-deprecating jokes about his age that he used on stage. "I'm so old, I have an autographed copy of the Bible," and "I'm so old my Social Security number is 3," are two of my favorites. He had another wonderful joke that I've repeated for years. "When I die, I want to die peacefully in my sleep, just like my grandfather. Not screaming and yelling like the passengers in his car."

Billy was one of the youngest old people I've ever known. But thinking of him does remind me of some great old-timer jokes.

> An old man marries a much younger woman. Unfortunately, their sex life leaves much to be desired. The man goes to his doctor. "No matter what I do," he explains, "my wife is unable to have an orgasm. Do you have any suggestions?" "I know of one thing that might work," says the doctor. "You have a swimming pool, don't you? The next time you make love to your wife, have the pool boy wave a towel over you. That should do the trick."
>
> The next afternoon, the man sees that Pedro the pool boy is cleaning the pool. He hands Pedro a towel and brings him up to the bedroom. As Pedro waves the towel, the man makes love to his wife. He works with every bit of energy he can muster, but at the end of

forty-five minutes the wife still hasn't had an orgasm.

The man is exhausted. He gets off the bed, grabs the towel, and says to Pedro, "Take over." Pedro drops his swim trunks, hops into bed, and, as the old man waves the towel, proceeds to screw the wife's brains out. She has a screaming orgasm that half the neighborhood can hear.

The old man says to Pedro, "You see. *That's* how you wave a towel."

*

An old man is sitting on a park bench, sobbing uncontrollably. Another man walks up to him. "What's the problem old-timer?" he asks.

"A week ago I got married to a twenty-two-year-old woman," he says. "Every day she cooks me the best meals you can imagine. And every night she makes inventive, enthusiastic, and passionate love to me. Sometimes we do it twice in one night."

"Well then, why are you crying?" asks the man.

"I can't remember where I live."

*

An old man goes into a confessional booth. "Forgive me father, for I have sinned," he says. "On Friday, I met two twenty-year old women. They came back with me to my apartment, and we spent the weekend engaged in a wide variety of sexual acts. They are back at my apartment waiting for me right now."

"Are you Catholic?" asks the priest. "No, I'm Jewish," says the old man.

"Then why are you telling me?" the priest asks.

"I'm telling everybody."

*

A very wealthy seventy-year-old man walks into his country club with a gorgeous young woman on his arm. When she leaves to go to the ladies room, some of his friends gather around him. "Is that your girlfriend?" they ask. "No, it's my wife," he replies.

"How in the world did you get a young, gorgeous woman like that to marry you?" they ask. "I lied about my age," he says.

"Did you tell her you were fifty?" they ask. "No, I told her I was ninety."

*

An elderly couple is in a lawyer's office. "We want to get a divorce," says the man. "My goodness," says the lawyer. "How old are you?" The man says, "I'm ninety-five, and she's ninety-three."

The lawyer asks, "Is there some type of incompatibility that has just arisen?" "Nope," says the man, "I've hated her guts for years." The woman chimes in, "And I could never stand this old bastard."

"Well then, why are you just now getting a divorce?"

"Oh," says the old man, "we wanted to wait until the kids were dead."

*

Hymie is one of the more notable characters at a retirement home near South Beach. Every morning he takes his constitutional, walking briskly around the grounds. On this particular morning, he sees Pincus. "Pincus," he says, "guess how old I am." "I don't know," says Pincus, "you look seventy-three or seventy-four." "Hah," says Hymie, "I'm eighty-two. Watch what you eat; take a walk every day; you could look this good, too."

Hymie continues his walk, and a few minutes later he runs into Shapiro. "Shapiro," he says, "guess how old I am." "It's hard to tell," says Shapiro. "You look like you're seventy-six or seventy-seven." "Hah," says Hymie. "I'm eighty-two. Get a little exercise; don't eat too much; you could look this good, too."

Hymie walks on, and eventually runs into Sadie. "Sadie, guess how old I am," he says. Sadie unzips his pants, reaches in, feels around for thirty seconds, takes her hand out, zips him up, and says, "You're eighty-two." "How could you know?" asks Hymie.

"I heard you tell Shapiro."

*

A man is visiting a friend who has had some medical problems. "You know, Morris, you are looking very happy these days," he says. "I am happy," says Morris. "My doctor has me on these pills that are really helping with my memory." "What's the name of the pills?" asks the friend.

"They're called…they're called. What's the name of the flower that's red and has a long stem?" "A rose?" says the friend.

"That's right. Hey, Rose! What's the name of that medicine I'm on?"

*

A man is celebrating his eightieth birthday with some friends. Unbeknownst to him, the friends have hired a hooker for him. The doorbell rings; the old man opens the door. A very provocatively dressed woman is standing on the front porch.

"Why are you here?" the old man asks. "I'm here to give you super sex," replies the hooker.

The old man thinks about it for a moment. "I'll take the soup."

*

An old man rings the doorbell at the whorehouse. The madam opens the door, sees the old man, and says, "What are you doing here, old-timer?" "I'm here for sex," says the old man. "You're here for sex?" says the madam. "For heaven's sake old man, you've had it."

"Oh," says the old man. "How much do I owe you?"

*

A man puts his father into a nursing home. He is conflicted over this decision, but his job makes it difficult to tend to his father at home. After getting his father settled in his new surroundings, the man leaves on a business trip. He returns a week later, and goes to visit his father. Looking through a window, he sees his father sitting in a chair in the day room. The door to the day room is locked, and there is no one to let the son in.

As the son watches through the window, his father begins to tilt to the right. He almost falls out of the chair he is sitting in, but a large attendant rushes over and straightens him up. A few minutes pass, and the father begins to tilt in the other direction. Again, an attendant hurries over and straightens him. Finally, someone unlocks the door for the son, and he enters the day room, pulling up a chair next to his father.

"So," says the son, "how is everything here, Dad? Do you like your room?" "Yeah, sure," says his father. "The room is fine." "Well, how about the food? Is the food good?" "Yeah, good food, sure." "You're making a few friends here, aren't you Dad? You've met some people; made friends?" "Friends, yeah, made some friends."

The son is becoming very concerned. "Well, gee Dad, what is it? What's wrong? You seem so sad."

"They won't let me fart."

[I love this joke, and I really pour my heart into it when I tell it. It's best to be seated when you tell the joke; I lean right and left, almost falling out of my chair. I also try to get some real emotion into the conversation between the father and son. The father is completely depressed about the situation; the son gets more concerned with each question. This is another great joke where the punch line falls on the last word, and comes out of nowhere.]

I didn't know Billy as well as I knew Jay Marshall. When I lived in the Midwest, Billy was on the west coast. After I moved to Las Vegas, I saw him more often. It was said of Billy that he had only one conversation in his life, and people just drifted in and out of it. I can confirm this. I'd see him at a convention and say, "Hello, Doctor." He'd say, "Hello, old son. I don't know why Al Koran was interested in that particular trick. It really didn't suit his act. We spoke about it, and I gave him some suggestions for other tricks, but he just wouldn't change his mind." I had no idea what the hell he was talking about, but I'd sit and listen just the same. Eventually we'd move on to other subjects, and when I left and someone else sat down to chat, they'd have no idea why Billy was talking about British jazz piano players.

The next two jokes take place in England. They remind me of Billy's dry sense of humor. I don't know if he told them, but I can certainly hear him telling them.

> A man from Essex is planning a three-week tour of Europe. He asks his brother to watch his house and feed his cat, Fluffy. The man is in Paris for a few days, and he calls his brother to make sure everything is all right. "How's Fluffy?" asks the man. "Fluffy's dead," says the brother. The man passes out from the shock of this news. He collapses on the street. A bystander calls an ambulance, and the man is admitted to a nearby hospital.
>
> The man is unconscious for two days. When he comes to, he calls his brother. "What are you, an idiot?" he shouts. "That's absolutely the wrong way to break bad news to someone." "What should I have done?" asks the brother.
>
> "You should have eased me into it. When I called the first time you should have said that the cat was on

the roof, and firemen were coming to get it down. The next time I called you should have said that the rescue was successful, but as the fireman came down the ladder with Fluffy he jumped from his arms and sprained his ankle. Then you should have told me that when the veterinarian checked him, he found that the ankle had been fractured, but he treated it, and Fluffy was moving around just fine. Then you should have told me that a small infection set in, but the vet was treating it with antibiotics. Then you should have said that the infection had spread, and that antibiotics were not going to work. The vet suggested that the most humane thing to do was to put Fluffy to sleep. He went peacefully and without pain."

"I'm really sorry," says the brother, "I didn't know."
"That's okay" says the man. "By the way, how's Mom?"

"She's on the roof."

*

Lord Elmsley is going on safari in Africa, and will be gone for several weeks. He puts his manservant, Jeeves, in charge of the manor. While on the hunt, the Lord is out of contact with the outside world. When he returns to Nairobi, he calls Jeeves. "How's everything at home?" he asks.

"Well sir," says Jeeves, "I have good news and I have bad news." "What's the bad news?" asks the Lord.

"Your hunting steed Challenger is dead, sir." "Challenger is dead? How did he die?"

"We believe he died of smoke inhalation." "Smoke inhalation? Smoke inhalation from what?"

"From the fire in the stable, sir." "A fire in the stable? How did that start?"

"We believe that a burning ember from the manor flew to the roof of the stable and set it on fire." "An ember from the manor? Are you telling me the manor burned down?"

"Yes, sir." "How in the world did that fire start?"

"We believe that one of the funeral candles fell over and caught the curtains on fire." "Funeral candles? What funeral candles?"

"The ones that were around your mother's coffin, sir." "My mother's coffin? Are you telling me that my mother is dead?"

"Yes, sir."

"So my mother is dead, the manor and the stable have burned to the ground, and my prize steed Challenger is dead. What could possibly be the good news?"

"Well, sir, due to the intense heat, the marigolds have bloomed a week early."

I'll wrap up this chapter with two more Billy McComb stories. I know the first story is true, because it happened at a convention I attended. The second story is probably not true, but Billy told it often, and it's so wonderful that I'll pretend it is. (Although Billy made an anonymous music hall performer the subject of the joke, I'll tell it as if it happened to him.)

Billy was attending a small magic convention in Canada. The attendees stayed in a boutique bed and breakfast hotel. Next to the hotel was a restaurant/bar that was frequented by college students. Billy and several of the magicians were seated around a picnic table in the main area of the bar. The bar was packed; the surrounding tables were jammed with college kids.

One of the students seated directly behind Billy let out a silent-but-deadly fart. The odor rose and floated over the table where Billy and the magicians were seated. Billy was in mid story. He stopped, sniffed the air, and said, "I think someone's doing my act."

Here's the second story. Years ago, when Billy was still working in the U.K., one of the tricks in his act was called Sands of the Desert; it used sand of three different colors. The method of the trick involved packing a handful of sand of each color into a condom, which was tied off, making a tight bundle. To produce the sand, the bundle was broken, and the sand poured out.

Billy was booked for a six-week run at a small theater. He did eight shows a week, and each show used up three of the sand bundles; for the length of the run he would need 144 bundles. Billy had arrived in the city on a Friday; the run began on Monday. Figuring that he could use the free days to prepare his props, he went to a drugstore and asked the pharmacist for a gross of condoms. The pharmacist's eyebrows rose slightly as he bagged the large box of prophylactics, but he said nothing.

Billy went back to his hotel room and spent the next two days preparing the bundles of sand for the trick. As he finished the last bunch, he noticed that the box was two condoms short. On Monday, he went back into the pharmacy and said to the druggist, "There were only 142 condoms in that box you sold me on Friday." "I'm very sorry," the druggist replied, "I hope I didn't ruin your weekend."

Chuck

It's tough to make a funny person laugh. Sometimes they don't laugh because they've heard the joke before. Sometimes, if you're making a situational joke, they don't laugh because they've been busy analyzing the situation, and they've already discovered the joke you just made up. Sometimes they actually think that what you've said is funny, but the only reaction they give is, "That's funny." Funny people have heard and said a lot of funny things in their lifetimes; if you want to get a real laugh out of them, you have to surprise them. Sometimes, the funny person is working on their own funny remark, and they aren't even paying attention. I remember a great joke about this.

> Every Friday, a group of comedy writers gets together for lunch at the Brown Derby in Hollywood. While they eat, the group swaps jokes, with each writer eagerly waiting to amuse the others with his latest bit of hilarity.
>
> One Friday, one of the regulars shows up a little late. He seems very preoccupied. "Is everything okay, Frank?" one of the group asks. "No, not really," says Frank. "My wife just called me. My mother-in-law has had a stroke. They've moved her into the intensive care unit at Mt. Sinai Hospital in Manhattan. She's stable, but it doesn't look good. I've got to run over to LAX and grab a plane to New York, but I don't think I'm going to get there before the old gal dies."
>
> Another writer says, "You think *that's* funny? These two Jews walk into a bar..."

I enjoy making Chuck Fayne laugh. It isn't easy. Chuck is a very funny man. He is also a wonderful close-up and stand-up magician, and a guy who knows the value of (for lack of a better word) stuff. For a while, Chuck had the third largest collection of ukuleles in the world. (It could be argued, of course, that had he wanted to be a real humanitarian, he would have cornered the market on accordions.) Chuck knows about antiques, collectibles, and other ephemera (that is, junk). When he lived in Los Angeles, Chuck would attend the Rose Bowl flea markets, which were held on the second Sunday of each month. Chuck would get to the stadium at 4:30 in the morning. He'd ride in with one of the vendors, and would spend the next three hours walking from booth to booth, scoping out each vendor's wares. He'd find items at one booth that he knew another vendor wanted. He'd buy at one vendor and sell at a profit to another vendor. By 8 a.m. when the swap meet officially opened, Chuck had finished his work and had headed home. Chuck's knowledge of what's available on the secondary market allowed him to pull off one of the greatest practical jokes of all time. You'll read about it later.

Chuck and I have several things in common. His father was a Russian Jew whose last name, Feinberg, was transformed into Fayne. This, of course, reminds me of a joke.

> In Indianapolis, there is a Chinese restaurant called The Happy Dragon. As you enter the restaurant, there's a picture of the four brothers who own it: Frankie Ting, Benny Ting, Charlie Ting, and Ole Olsen. I was intrigued by the name of the fourth brother, so I asked my waiter about it.
>
> Apparently, when the four brothers arrived in the United States from China, they got separated at the immigration counter; three of the brothers were in one line, the other was in another line. A Swede, Ole Olsen, stood in line in front of the fourth brother. When he had finished and left, the immigration officer asked the fourth brother, "What's your name?" He replied, "Sam Ting."

That fact that Chuck and I share a Jewish heritage reminded me that I haven't included a section of Jewish jokes in this collection. Let's make up for that now.

A salesman is in Scotland on business. One day, he has a free afternoon and walks into a fabric shop in Glasgow. There he finds a gorgeous piece of wool that would make a beautiful suit. Unfortunately, the piece of fabric is a remnant on the bolt, and he isn't sure that there's enough fabric for a suit. He buys the cloth anyway, and takes it home with him.

On his first day back to work in New York City, he gets off the subway a few stops early, in the garment district. He has the cloth with him, and walks into a tailor shop. "I bought this fabric in Scotland," he tells the Jewish tailor. "Is there enough here to make a suit?" "I don't know," says the tailor, "we'll have to measure." The tailor measures the man and he measures the cloth. "I'm sorry," he says, "but there's not enough fabric."

The man is discouraged by the news. He leaves the tailor shop and begins walking toward the next subway stop. On the way, he passes a second tailor shop. Thinking that it can't hurt to get a second opinion, he goes in and explains the situation to the tailor. The tailor measures him, measures the cloth, and tells him to come back in two weeks.

When the man returns two weeks later, the tailor presents him with a beautiful three-piece suit made from the fabric. The man tries it on, and while he's admiring himself in the mirror, the tailor's four-year-old son walks out wearing a miniature version of the suit. The man is dumbfounded. He pays for the suit and walks back to the first tailor's shop.

"Do you remember me? I was in here two weeks ago. You said you couldn't make a suit from the fabric I had. I walked down the street to another shop. The tailor there not only made me a three-piece suit, he had enough fabric left over to make his four-year-old son a suit. What's the deal?

The tailor replies, "My son is twelve."

*

Two rabbis are talking. They each notice that their

suits have become old and threadbare. One says, "My nephew Pincus is a tailor. We should visit him; he'll give us a good deal." They call Pincus. "Yes, Uncle, come right over. I have some beautiful suits for you, and I'll give you such a deal on them."

What the rabbis don't know is that Pincus has two dark-blue suits that he has been unable to sell. When the rabbis arrive, Pincus shows them the suits. "Well, these are nice suits," says one rabbi, "but we wear black suits. These are blue suits." "No, no, Uncle," says Pincus, "these are black suits. The front window is dirty, and the light comes in funny. Try on the suits; I know you'll love them."

The rabbis try on the suits; they fit perfectly. As the rabbis check their reflections in the store mirror one says, "They are very nice suits, Pincus, and they fit very well, but these are blue suits. We need black suits." "No, Uncle," says Pincus, "the florescent lights in the store give a false impression. Buy the suits; I'll make you such a deal on them."

So, the rabbis buy the suits, and they walk out of the store wearing them. One rabbi says, "Out here in the daylight, I could swear that these are blue suits. Wait a minute; there are a couple of nuns over there. They always wear black. Let's go stand by them and we'll check."

The rabbis walk over to the nuns, speak with them for a moment, and then walk away. "Now wasn't that nice," says one nun. "Two men of a different faith come to talk with us. And they even spoke a little Latin, too." "Yes," says the other, "but my Latin must be a bit rusty. What does, 'Ah, Pincus fucked us' mean?"

*

Two Jewish fellows read in the paper that a local Catholic church is giving $500 to anyone who converts to Catholicism. "This is great," says one of them. "We'll go down to the church, pretend to convert, and make $500 each for doing nothing."

They walk down to the church. "I'll go in first," says

one man. "You wait for me here. When I come out, you can go in. That way they won't think we're together." The first man goes into the church. He is gone for a long time. Six hours pass; finally the man comes out of the church. "Did you get the money?" his friend asks.

"*Money*? Is that *all* you people think about?"

*

Two men are having lunch. One says, "Here's a great joke. These two Jews are..." "Wait a minute," says his friend. "Why does it always have to be Jews?" "It doesn't have to be Jews," says the first man. "It could be Chinamen." "Okay, then, make it Chinamen."

"So, these two Chinamen are on their way to Temple..."

*

A rabbi desperately wants to win the lottery. Every Saturday he prays fervently to God to allow him to win the lottery. But every Monday, when the numbers are drawn, he is disappointed. After several months of this, the rabbi becomes frustrated. His prayers are full of anger. "God, why won't you let me win the lottery?" Just then, a large cloud appears above the rabbi's head. The cloud opens, and the face of God appears. God says, "Hey, meet me halfway. Buy a ticket."

*

Two Jewish men are talking. One says, "I need to get dentures. Do you know of a reasonably priced dentist?" The second man says, "My nephew Morris is a dentist. He can make you a marvelous set of dentures that won't cost an arm and a leg. Go see him. Mention my name; he'll make you such a deal."

The first man goes to see Morris the dentist. Six weeks pass; the two men meet up again. "So, I heard that you went to see Morris and he made you the dentures. How are they working out?" The friend replies, "Two days ago, I was in Central Park. I decided to rent a row boat and row around the lake. As I was getting into the boat, I slipped. One of my legs went outside of the boat, into the water; the other leg stayed inside. My balls got caught in the oarlock. And that was the first time in six weeks that my teeth didn't hurt."

*

A little Jewish man eats lunch every day at a deli near his apartment. Every day he orders a hot bowl of borscht. He has done this for so many years, that the restaurant simply has the soup ready for him at his favorite table.

One day, the man sits down, looks at the borscht, and calls over a waiter. "Taste the borscht," he says to the waiter. "What's wrong with the borscht?" asks the waiter. "Taste the borscht," says the man. "The borscht has cooled off; I'll bring you a fresh bowl," says the waiter. "Taste the borscht." "You didn't want borscht today; you wanted something else. Tell me what you want; I'll bring it to you, no charge." "Taste the borscht," says the man. "Okay, okay, I'll taste the borscht…where's the spoon?"

The man says, "Ahhh…"

This is a little off subject, but here's another fine waiter joke.

A man and his wife go to a trendy, new restaurant. The restaurant prides itself on its cleanliness. The glassware sparkles, the plates and cutlery shine, and the floor looks clean enough to eat from. When the waiter comes to the table, the man comments on how amazingly sanitary the restaurant is.

"Yes sir," says the waiter. "We believe we have implemented measures above and beyond those of any other restaurant. Do you see the tongs hanging around my neck? We serve all the food with those tongs; human hands never touch your food. Do you see the string attached to my zipper? When I use the rest room, I pull that string; it opens my fly and automatically removes my member."

"That's remarkable," says the man. "But wait a minute. How do you put it back in your pants when you're done?"

"I don't know about the other waiters, but I use my tongs."

I have heard and told many Jewish jokes over the years, but I have only heard one really good Gentile joke. It goes like this.

A Gentile calls his mother from work. "Hi, Mom," he says. "I know that I was supposed to come over and have dinner with you tonight, and I know we haven't seen each other in a while, but I have a very important presentation tomorrow and I have to finish it up tonight. So, I won't be able to come over for dinner."

The mother says, "Okay."

And to be fair, here are some other really good religious jokes.

*

A man is standing on the railing of a bridge, preparing to jump to his death. A passerby sees him and runs over. "Don't do it, friend. Don't jump. Things can't be that bad." "They are that bad," says the man on the railing. "My business is failing. I'm going to lose everything that I worked my tail off for, plus my house, my car, and all my belongings. There's no other way but to jump."

"Listen to me friend; here's what I want you to do," says the passerby. "There's a hotel over there. Get a room. In the nightstand by the bed is a Bible. I want you to open the Bible to a random page, close your eyes, and put your finger down somewhere on the page. God will show you the path that you must take."

The man steps down off the railing and walks to the hotel. A year passes. By a coincidence, the Good Samaritan and the man meet each other on the street. The man looks wonderful. He's dressed in a thousand-dollar suit and is wearing a Rolex. "You look just great; I assume you took my advice."

"Yes I did," says the wealthy man. "I got the room, opened up the Bible, put my finger down, and got the advice I needed." "Really. What did it say?"

"Chapter 11."

*

A man goes to confession. "Father," he says, "I have a very difficult and delicate situation to discuss with you." "Yes, my son," says the priest, "go on, go on." "Well, for the past several years my wife and I have been unable to have sexual relations. I don't want to go into the reasons for this; I'll just say that we accepted the situation, and simply put that aspect of our married life out of our minds." "Yes, my son, go on, go on."

"Today, my wife was bent over a sack of potatoes, about to pick it up. And the sight of her, bent over like that, brought to me a feeling that I hadn't had for so many years. I was like a maddened bull. I grabbed her, and when I did, she felt the passion rising within her. We ripped off our clothes and made ecstatic, passionate love, right there on the sack of potatoes. And I thought I should come to you."

"But why, my son? There is nothing wrong here. For one reason or another you and your wife were unable to have sex, and the simple act of bending over a sack of potatoes rekindled the virility in you and the passion in her. This is a beautiful thing; this is a blessed thing. Why did you think you should come to me?"

"I thought they would throw us out of the church," says the man. "Why would we throw you out of the church?" the priest asks.

"Well, they threw us out of the supermarket."

[When telling this joke, use the name of a supermarket familiar to your area.]

*

A man visits the minister of his church at his office one Monday morning. "I need you to do me a favor," he says. "After the service yesterday, someone walked off with my hat. Next Sunday will you do a sermon on the Ten Commandments? I'll hide up above the choir loft and watch the congregation. When you get to 'Thou shall not steal' someone will look guilty, and I'll know who took my hat."

The minister agrees. The next Sunday, the minister gives a rousing sermon on the Ten Commandments. After the service, the minister sees the man leaving the church. "Did you spot the guilty party?" asks the minister. "Actually," says the man, "when you got to the part about 'Thou shall not commit adultery,' I remembered where I left my hat."

*

A man has been stranded on an island for many years. One day, a passing ship spots a fire he has kept burning on the beach. The ship sends a boat to pick up the man.

When the rescue party gets to the island, they see that the man has built three huts. "Why are there three huts?" asks one of the crew. "Well," says the man, "the first hut is the one I sleep in; the second hut is the church I go to." "What about the third hut?"

"That's the church I *used* to go to."

*

The weather department has forecast severe storms for the area around a small town in Missouri. There is a possibility of floods. A man is standing in front of his house. A police car drives by. "Get in," says a policeman. "We'll take you to safety." "No need," says the man. "God will provide for me."

The rain starts; the water rises. The man climbs on the roof of his house. Two Red Cross workers come by in a boat. "Get in the boat," one says. "We'll take you to safety." "No need," says the man. "God will save me."

The waters continue to rise, covering the man up to his neck. A National Guard helicopter flies over. It drops a ladder down to the man. One of the guardsmen yells, "Climb up the ladder, and we'll get you out of here." "No need," says the man. "God will take care of me." The helicopter flies away. The water climbs higher, covering the man's head. He drowns.

When he awakes, he is in heaven standing before God. "Why didn't you help me?" asks the man. "What are you talking about?" replies God. "I sent a police car, a boat, and a helicopter."

*

A man has driven downtown for an important meeting. Unfortunately, he can't find a single parking space. He's starting to get frantic, because if he's late for the meeting the whole deal will go south. He drives around desperately looking for a parking space, and he begins to panic.

"God," the man says, "please get me a parking space. If you do, I'll go to church every Sunday, I'll tithe twenty percent of my income, and I'll do thirty hours of community service a week." Just then, a car backs out of a parking space.

He looks heavenward and says, "Never mind. This guy's leaving."

*

Jebediah is a sharecropper. He lives in a small shack; its only piece of furniture is a bed frame with a worn mattress. Hidden in the mattress is the small amount of money Jebediah has saved over the years. Five miles from the shack is a patch of land that Jebediah sharecrops. Every morning he hitches up his mule, walks five miles, and works the land. Every evening he walks back, cooks a simple meal over an open fire, and goes to sleep on his bare mattress.

One morning, Jebediah and the mule walk to the field. When they get there, they see that locusts have attacked the crop; the vegetation has been stripped to the ground. Jebediah decides that there is nothing more to be done, so he and the mule start to walk back to the shack. The mule takes three steps and falls over dead. Jebediah loved that mule, so he drags the mule all the way back to the shack. When he gets to the shack, he sees that lightning has struck; the shack has burned to the ground, and all of Jebediah's meager possessions, including the money he has saved, are now ashes.

Jebediah is overwhelmed with grief and anger. He shouts to the heavens, "God! Are you listening to me, God? I want to talk to you!" Just then, a large cloud forms on the ground, and from out of the cloud steps God. "Yes, Jebediah, what can I do for you?" asks God.

"I want to know why, God. I don't understand you. I've never hurt anyone in my life. All I've ever tried to do is eke out a living. But today you sent locusts to destroy my crop. Then you struck down my mule. I loved that mule, God, and you killed it. And when I got home, I saw that you tossed a lightning bolt to burn down my shack, my bed, and my money. So I have to ask why, God; why did you do all these things to me?"

And God replies, "I don't know, Jebediah. There's just something about you that pisses me off."

Another thing Chuck and I share is that we both became fathers late in life. When Chuck's children were very young, he discussed this in his act. "I'm the father of two young children," he would say. "By the time they're out of diapers, I'll be in them. Incidentally, the people who make disposable diapers do not tell the truth about their product. On the box it says 'ten to fourteen pounds.' That's a lie; they can't nearly hold that much." Since Chuck's children are now teenagers, he has no use for the lines, and I'm happy to appropriate them.

I have been thinking about jokes that will make my daughter laugh when she is old enough to understand English (and jokes), so I've been collecting silly clean jokes.

A bear walks into a bar. The bartender says, "What would you like to drink?" The bear says, "Let me have a gin and [long pause] tonic." The bartender says,

"Why the big pause?"

The bear says, "I don't know. My Dad had big paws."

[Okay, okay. So I'll probably have to wait a few years before I tell that one.]

*

A chicken walks into a library and says to the librarian, "Book, book, book." The librarian gives the chicken a book. The chicken leaves the library with the book. A few hours later, it walks back in, drops the book on the floor, and says to the librarian, "Book, book, book." The librarian gives a different book to the chicken. The chicken leaves with the book.

A few more hours pass, and the chicken walks in carrying the book. It drops the book on the floor and says to the librarian, "Book, book, book." The librarian gives the chicken a third book. This time, when the chicken leaves the library with the book, the librarian follows. The chicken walks out of the city, down a dirt road, and onto a small lane. The lane leads past a farmhouse, into a meadow, and dead ends at a large pond. A big bullfrog sits on the edge of the pond. The chicken drops the book in front of the frog and says, "Book, book, book."

The frog says, "Read it, read it."

["Book, book, book" should sound like clucking.]

*

A panda bear walks into a restaurant. He sits down, orders a meal, and eats it. The waiter brings the check. "What's this?" asks the panda. "It's the bill for your meal," says the waiter. "I'm a panda; look it up," says the panda. "I don't care what you are," says the waiter. "You ate the food; you have to pay the check."

The panda pulls out a gun, fires three shots into the ceiling, and starts to leave the restaurant. The maitre d' stops him. "Where do you think you're going?" he asks the panda. "I'm a panda; look it up," says the panda. The maitre d' pulls out a dictionary. He flips through it, reads something, and says, "Okay, you can go." The panda walks out of the restaurant.

The waiter says to the maitre d', "Why did you let him go?" The maitre d' hands the waiter the dictionary, and he reads, "Panda: a large bear from Asia. Eats shoots and leaves."

*

A duck walks into a convenience store. "Do you have any plums?" he asks the clerk. "No," says the clerk. "This is a convenience store; we don't carry any fruits or vegetables." The duck leaves.

The next day, the duck returns. "Do you have any plums?" he asks the clerk. "No. This is a convenience store." The duck leaves.

The duck returns the next day. "Do you have any plums?" "No," says the clerk, "and I'm getting real tired of this. If you come in and ask for plums again, I'm going to nail your stupid webbed feet to the floor." The duck leaves.

The next day, the duck returns to the convenience store. The clerk holds his breath. "Do you have any nails?" asks the duck. The clerk breathes a sigh of relief. "No," he says. "Great," says the duck. "Do you have any plums?"

*

A couple goes to a very fancy restaurant. The man says to the maitre d', "We'd like a table by the window, and would you please tell our waiter to bring a bottle of your finest champagne when he delivers the menus."

The couple is seated, and a few minutes later the waiter brings the bottle of champagne. "Are you celebrating something this evening – a birthday or an anniversary?" "Yes, we are celebrating," says the man, but it's neither of those things. Today we finished a jigsaw puzzle." "Really," says the waiter.

"Yes," says the man, "we've been working on it for eighteen months; this afternoon we put in the final piece, and I said to my wife, 'Tonight we celebrate.'" "Well, that's quite an accomplishment," says the waiter.

"You better believe it," says the man. "The box said, 'Four to Six Years'."

*

Q: What did the snail say when it jumped on the turtle's back?
A: Wheeee!

*

A snail is mugged by two turtles. The police arrive. "Tell us exactly what happened," says one of the policemen. "I don't know if I can," says the snail. "It all happened so fast."

Although the following joke is not one that I'd tell to my daughter anytime in the foreseeable future, the previous jokes reminded me of it.

A man sees a little boy sitting in a red wagon being pulled by a dog. The boy is wearing a fireman's hat. He walks up to the boy. "You know, young man," he says, "if you tie the rope around the dog's neck instead of his testicles, he'll pull you faster."

"Yeah," says the boy, "but then I lose my siren."

Although Chuck and I had known each other for several years, we really became close friends when we worked a magic convention in Australia. This was the type of convention that produces camaraderie, especially between two foreigners who are far from home. Chuck and I got suckered into doing some awful things. We wasted a full afternoon appearing on an Australian talk show. (My job was to provide information about the big Saturday night gala show. The interview ran long and the host never asked me about it.) For some reason, I was the final act of an all-female after-banquet show. And poor Chuck was the emcee of an evening show that ran for more than four hours. I was supposed to be on the show, but, because of jet lag, I fell asleep standing against a wall backstage. When I woke up, about three hours into the show, I heard Chuck make the following introduction, "I don't know who this guy is; I don't know what he does; but he's one of my favorites. Please welcome..."

That reminds me of some show-business jokes.

> A juggler gets a gig with the Ringling Brothers Circus. As he's driving to his first performance, he's pulled over by a cop for speeding. "What's the big hurry?" asks the policeman. "Actually, officer, I'm a juggler and I'm on my way to my first performance with the Ringling Brothers Circus. I'm running a little late, and I guess I didn't watch my speed." "A juggler?" says the cop. "I love jugglers. Juggle something for me." "All of my equipment is at the arena. I don't have anything with me that I could juggle." "Could you juggle three road flares?" asks the cop. "I suppose so."
>
> The policeman opens the trunk of his patrol car and brings out three flares. The juggler takes them and starts doing various patterns. As he is doing this, another car pulls up behind the police car. A drunk gets out and walks up to the cop.
>
> "You might as well arrest me," he says to the cop. "There's no way I could pass *that* test."

*

> A midget lives on the twentieth floor of an apartment building. One evening he gets in to the elevator with several other people. Immediately, a rancid smell of feces and urine is noticeable. It's coming from the midget. He notices the stares of the other passengers. "I'm sorry," he says. "I work at the circus. My job is to wash down the elephants before they go into the ring. When I do that they sometimes piss and crap on me."

"That's horrible," says one of the passengers. "Why don't you find another job?"

"What, and give up show business?"

*

A man is desperate for work. He gets a job at the circus. His job is to purge the circus' three elephants before they go out to the center ring. Holding a broom handle, he enters the elephant pen and walks behind a two-year-old elephant that has just joined the circus. He jams the broom handle up the elephant's rear end. The elephant rears back on its hind legs and lets out a trumpeting roar. He swings his head and knocks the man on his ass.

The second elephant is five-years old and has been with the circus for two years. When the man sticks the broom up the elephant's rear end, it lets out a roar and kicks back with its hind legs. The man barely avoids getting hit. The man runs over to the third elephant, which has been with the circus for twenty years. He sticks the broom handle up the elephant's ass. The elephant turns his head and asks, "How's the crowd tonight?"

[Before you tell this joke, tell your audience not to interrupt you. When you start, some people may think you are going to tell the "get out of show business" joke. That joke is fairly well known. The one above is not.]

*

A man walks into a talent agent's office. "I'm not in the show business, you know," he says to the agent. "I'm a construction worker. But I think I may have some sort of special ability. Last week, I was on the building site, and the guy working the crane swung a girder around and hit me in the head with it. And it had no effect on me whatsoever. It just like, bounced off, you know? And this morning, I had bent over to pick up my lunch box, and my hard hat fell off. Just then, a guy two floors above me dropped a bucket of rivets. It hit me on the top of my head, and it didn't hurt me it all.

It's like my head is made of steel or something.

"So I was thinking that I could work carnivals and fairs, and bill myself as 'Mr. Hard Head.' Kids could throw baseballs or bricks or something, and they would just bounce off. So what do you think?"

"This is not really the type of talent I book," says the agent. "I'm not sure that I'm the one to help you..."

"No, no, you've got to see me do this," says the man. He grabs an autographed Johnny Bench baseball bat that the agent has hanging on his wall. "Here, hit me in the head with this. Hit me as hard as you can. It won't bother me at all. You have to see this."

"I can't hit you with a baseball bat," says the agent. But the man puts the bat in his hands. "Swing away; swing away," says the man. The agent decides that the only way to get rid of the guy is to comply, so he taps him on the head with the bat.

The construction worker goes down in a heap. He's out cold. The agent tries to rouse him. No luck – the guy is unconscious. Now the agent is panicked. He hit the man with a bat; that's assault with a deadly weapon. He calls 911. When the ambulance arrives, he rides with the man to the hospital. He stays with him as he's examined in the emergency room. The man remains unconscious. The agent insists that they put the construction worker in a private room. The agent stays with the man for the next forty-eight hours. He sits by the bed; he pees in a cup. He never leaves. He decides that the first person the construction workers sees when he wakes up has to be him, so he can explain the situation and avoid a lawsuit or worse.

Sixty hours after he was hit, the construction worker stirs. The agent gets up and stands next to him. The man opens his eyes and sits up in bed. He sees the agent and says, "Ta dah!"

*

Cecil B. DeMille is shooting a huge action sequence. Barbarian hordes are going to ride into a village and burn it to the ground. The scene involves hundreds of extras and stuntmen. The set will be destroyed at the end of the sequence, making this a one-time event.

Five cameramen are scattered around. Two are stationed within the village, one is mounted on a horse, another is on a track that winds around the village, the fifth camera is on a hilltop, capturing the wide shot.

DeMille yells, "Action!" The barbarians ride into the village. There is simulated death, and actual destruction. The entire town goes up in flames.

DeMille yells, "Cut." He gets on his walkie-talkie. "How was that, camera one?" he asks. "I'm sorry, C.B.," answers the cameraman. "Our film broke just as the shot started. We didn't get anything."

"How about you, camera two?" "Sorry, C.B., a horse threw up a rock and cracked our lens. We didn't get anything."

"Camera three, what about you?" "I fell off my horse, C.B. The camera was crushed."

"Camera four, did you get anything?" "No, C.B. The dolly jammed on the track. When we tried to free it, we flipped over the camera."

DeMille is frantic. "Camera five, what about you?" The cameraman replies, "Ready when you are, C.B."

Then there are jokes about joke tellers.

Bob invites Jim to spend an afternoon at his country club. They are sitting in the bar when someone yells out, "Eighty-one." Everyone in the bar laughs. A few minutes later, someone shouts, "Twelve," and everyone laughs heartily. Then someone shouts out, "Sixty-four." There is dead silence in the bar.

Jim is completely puzzled. "What's going on?" he asks Bob. "All of us at the country club have told jokes for many years," says Bob. "To save time we just numbered the punch lines." "How come nobody laughed when the guy shouted 'Sixty-four'?"

"Some people just don't know how to tell a joke."

*

Bob invites Jim to spend an afternoon at his country club. They are sitting in the bar when someone yells out, "Eighty-one." Everyone in the bar laughs. A few minutes later, someone shouts, "Twelve," and everyone laughs heartily. Then someone shouts out, "Sixty-four." Everyone in the bar falls on the ground laughing.

Jim is completely puzzled. "What's going on?" he asks Bob. "All of us at the country club have told jokes for many years. To save time we just numbered the punch lines." "Why did everybody laugh so hard when the guy shouted 'Sixty-four'?"

"We hadn't heard that one before."

[Here again are two jokes with similar set-ups but different punch lines. The first joke is more familiar. In my experience, even well-versed joke tellers are unaware of the second joke. I prefer the second one. The punch line is unexpected and surreal.]

*

A comic has finished his shows at a local comedy club and is sitting in his hotel room watching television. His phone rings. "Hi," says a very sexy voice, "I'm really sorry to bother you, but I was at the Laugh Factory tonight. I think you are the funniest man I have ever seen, and I find that to be incredibly attractive. If it's okay with you, I'd like to come up to your room and pleasure you in ways you can't even imagine. I'll give you a night that you'll remember for the rest of your life."

The comic says, "Were you at the first or the second show?"

And then there are jokes specifically geared to tell to joke tellers.

A comic is driving around Los Angeles. This guy is the hottest comic in America. He's done Leno; he's done Letterman; and he's killed both times. His career is about to take off like a rocket. His cell phone rings; it's his agent. "Listen," says the agent, "are you anywhere near the L.A. Convention Center?" "Actually," says the comic, "I'm about four minutes away." "Is there any way you can get over there right now and head to Ballroom C? The comic I hired as the after-dinner entertainment ate some of the banquet food and is sick as a dog. The people in the ballroom are waiting for someone to entertain them. Just walk in, go up on the stage, and start. I'll owe you one if you can help me out here."

The comic says no problem. He speeds over to the convention center, valet parks his car, races to the ballroom, and charges up on stage. He launches into his A material.

Nothing – not a peep, not a chuckle, not a titter comes from the audience. After a minute, a large bead of sweat starts to run down his cheek. After three minutes of performing to dead silence, his face is covered with sweat. After six minutes, he's soaked like a wet rag.

Just then, his eyes adjust to the spotlight, and he notices a large banner that stretches across the back of the ballroom. It reads, "Saludos a Nuestros Amigos de Mexico." The comic stops and looks around the audience. "Excuse me," he says, "does anyone in the room understand English?" One man raises his hand.

"Well then, fuck *you*."

[I'll tell you right now, if you tell this joke to a doctor, a lawyer, an accountant, or anyone else who's not in show business, you won't get a laugh. But tell it to anyone who has ever stood in front of audience and tried to entertain them, and you'll get roars. There is a scene in Albert Brooks' movie *Looking for Comedy in the Muslim World* that completely cracked me up. I thought Brooks was going to do this gag. He was performing for a group of East Indians, and no one was laughing. He asked if anyone understood English, and *everyone* raised their hands.]

*

A man walks into a tavern and sits down at the bar. He is well dressed and appears normal except for the fact that he has a big orange head. He orders a scotch. When the drink comes, the man pulls out a wallet that is full of hundred-dollar bills. He tosses one on the bar and tells the bartender to keep the change. He drinks for a while. Finally, the bartender's curiosity overwhelms him. "What's with the big orange head?" he asks the man.

"I was walking on the beach one morning," the man says. "My toe hit something hard. When I dug it out of the sand, it turned out to be an old brass lamp. I rubbed it on my shirt to polish it up a bit, and a very old genie came out. He said he would grant me three wishes. The first thing I wished for was to be rich. You see this wallet? It's always filled with hundred-dollar bills. And then I wished to spend a weekend with the Dallas Cowboys cheerleaders. Poof, I was in a penthouse apartment in New York City with all of them, naked as the day they were born.

"And then, I fucked up and wished for a big orange head."

[What makes this joke funny is that when you tell it to a joke teller they will completely stop paying attention to the joke as they try to figure out what the man could have possibly said that the old genii misinterpreted as "big orange head." You'll have to pick your audience carefully, but with the right recipient you'll get a big laugh.]

I heard the Big Orange Head joke from Penn Jillette, and I immediately told it to Mac King (a terrific comedy magician who lives in Vegas). Penn was a little upset, because *he* had wanted to tell the joke to Mac. I understand Penn's feelings; when you hear a new joke, you want to be the first to tell it to your friends, especially a joke like the Big Orange Head, which has limited audience appeal.

This reminds me that in 1984 I was part of a cabaret show at an I.B.M. convention in Norfolk, Virginia. Also on the bill were Jay Marshall, Allan Hayden, and Bob Sheets, funny men all. As part of my segment, I admonished the audience to keep the jokes they heard to themselves. I asked that they not repeat the jokes to their friends at the convention. We had to repeat the show three times, and if the audience went out and told the jokes they heard in the show to the other conventioneers, we wouldn't get many laughs during the last two shows.

I was at the bar the evening after the first cabaret show. A guy walked up to me and said, "I heard a great joke today. This guy walks into a bar, and he looks like this..." He was starting to tell me the "Sears" joke that I had used as part of my cabaret act. "That's a joke I used during the cabaret show today," I told him. "Were you at the show?" "No, I'm going to the show on Saturday," he replied. "Then who told you the joke?" I asked, angry that someone would blatantly ignore my request for secrecy. The man replied, "Jay Marshall."

I mentioned earlier that Chuck was responsible for the most ingenious and insidious practical joke I have ever heard. Here it is. Chuck had a friend who had purchased a beautiful old house in Los Angeles. The friend was refurbishing the house, and as the first step in that process was restoring twelve doors. Each of these doors had distinctive, very unusual crystal doorknobs, which, like the house, were made in the 1920s. The owner had removed the twelve sets of doorknobs and placed them on the dining-room table. He then removed all the doors and took them out to the garage to refinish them.

Chuck stopped by shortly after this process started, and he noticed the pile of doorknobs on the dining room table. Chuck knew where he could find *another* set of doorknobs that matched exactly. So, the next day Chuck bought a pair of doorknobs, returned to the friend's house, and secretly added them to the pile on the table.

After several months, when the friend had finished restoring all the doors, had hung them all, and had reattached the hardware, there were still two doorknobs on the table. But the friend didn't think he had gained two doorknobs; he thought he had *misplaced* a door. As I type this up, the beauty of this prank gives me goose bumps.

Chuck Fayne is a show-business veteran. One day we were talking about the worst introductions we'd ever had. Mine occurred at a close-up show at a magic convention in Florida. The host in the performance room stood up, looked at his watch, and said, "Well, we have one more guy before lunch." That was it. Chuck had two stories that easily topped mine.

Chuck was hired to perform at a big party for the Los Angeles Police Department. It was a rousing party; the alcohol flowed freely. Chuck was scheduled to do his stage act. When it came time to perform, the chief of police, who was well buttered, came out and introduced Chuck this way: "Ladies and gentlemen, we have a special treat tonight: a man who has been honored many times by the Magic Castle in Hollywood. Please give a warm welcome to the amazing and very funny – Fuck Chain." Chuck, of course, referred to himself that way for the entire show.

Another time, Chuck was working a party at the Ambassador Hotel. The party was a celebration for the CEO of an accounting firm who was retiring. There were rumors that the man was retiring for health reasons, but no one knew for sure. Chuck was seated at the dais. After dinner, the CEO stood up and addressed the guests. "I want to thank all of you for being here this evening," he said. "All of you have stuck with me through thick and thin. You have made this company what it is today. I want to put all the rumors to rest. I have AIDS. Because of this, I am retiring and I am leaving the day-to-day operation of the company to Frank, my dear friend and business associate of twenty-five years. I don't know how much time I have left, but however much time that is, I am going to spend it enjoying life with my family and friends...And now, the comedy magic of Chuck Fayne."

Chuck stood up and addressed the guests, who were still in a state of shocked disbelief. He said, "I, too, must lay all rumors to rest. I didn't give it to him."

Bob

There are no "joke" jokes in this chapter. I just need to spend a few pages to tell you about Bob Read. Bob was the funniest person I've ever known. When I remember the times I laughed so hard that the tears ran down my leg, Bob was there. He should have been a star; he should have been famous. But he never could have been, because to be famous today, you have to be good on TV, and, for several reasons, Bob couldn't do what he did on TV. First, you had to see him in person. With Bob, you didn't just watch the show; you were part of the show. Bob liked to have his audience near him. (For that reason, he loved performing in pubs.) He liked to keep his eyes on you, just in case you did or said something that he could riff on. When he worked, Bob was like a jungle animal sniffing out prey, except Bob was sniffing out laughs.

Bob was a "part-time pro." His "real" job was as a representative for the wool industry, a gig that often brought him to the United States. I first met him in the late 1970s, in Chicago, while visiting Jay Marshall. When I arrived at the shop, Jay said to me, "You're lucky. Bob Read's in town. We're going to have dinner with him tonight." At the time, I had only a vague idea of who Bob Read was. "You'll like him," said Jay. "He's really funny." Coming from Jay Marshall, the words "he's really funny" were a high compliment.

Bob was a dapper man of medium height. He had a twinkle in his eye. That evening, I heard Bob tell the story of how he got trapped, naked, in the master bedroom of his own house, and had to tie together bed sheets to effect his escape. There was much more to the story than that, of course; the telling of it ran to twenty minutes. As is so often the case when I think about Bob in action, I find that the details are hazy; I can remember the main point, but everything else is obscured with laughter. We didn't do any magic that first night, but we all laughed a lot.

Bob wasn't really a joke teller, but he was a marvelous storyteller. His stories were (mostly) true-to-life adventures. When Bob found himself in a crazy situation, his first thought would be, "I could get five minutes out of this." (Although what Bob thought was five minutes was usually twenty minutes.) For that reason, I think that the crazier life got, the better Bob liked it. It wasn't as easy for those around him. Lisa and I stayed with Bob and his wife Pauline in October of 2005. Bob and Pauline had recently returned from a vacation in Italy, exploring the country by car. At breakfast one morning, Bob told us the story of how they had become hopelessly lost during an afternoon drive. Road signs were either nonexistent, or they pointed in the wrong directions. The situation became more frustrating and infuriating. After several hours of aimless driving, Bob said to Pauline, "I could get five minutes out of this." She replied, "Not here you can't."

In addition to being a great performer, Bob was a serious magic historian. He was the world's foremost expert on the history of the cups and balls as depicted in prints and other works of art. (He was actively preparing a major book on this subject.) His home housed an amazing collection of artifacts, including a set of cups once owned by Johann Nepomuk Hofzinser, an important nineteenth century Viennese conjuror. Bob was happy to show off his collection, and even allowed visitors to handle the famous Hofzinser cups. (Teller writes of his experience with these cups in *Penn & Teller's How to Play in Traffic*.)

During the five days we stayed at the Read home, Bob was busy preparing a talk he would give in November at the Los Angeles Conference on Magic History. He was going to incorporate PowerPoint into his presentation, and Lisa showed him some of the cool features of the program. I could tell that Bob was excited about the technology, but the twinkle in his eye told me that what he was really excited about were the comedic possibilities.

Bob drove Lisa and me from his home in Harrow to Watford, where I was going to give a lecture. Bob took city streets, because he didn't like driving on the M1. We were in Bob's Jaguar, which didn't have a radio because someone stole it. And, yes, Bob got five minutes out of that situation. When we got to Watford, Bob said, "You have to be careful here, if you make a wrong turn, you're on the M1 headed back to London." As he said "M1" we discovered that we were, indeed, on the M1, driving back to London, a situation that even I could get five minutes out of.

When Bob did his act, he moved like Gene Kelly. He rarely stood still, floating around the crowd, drawing everyone into the performance. He believed that good magic began in the feet; he often mentioned this in his magic lectures. In fact, Bob had a method for producing a wine bottle from a handkerchief that was totally accomplished through choreography. He would perform it in his lectures, and it would fool every magician in the room. Then he would explain it, and, an hour later, do it again and fool everyone all over again.

Bob had a magic lecture unlike any I have ever seen (and I have seen a lot of them). During the first half, he performed his effects, and he had you laughing until you couldn't breathe. In the second half, he'd explain the tricks, accompanied by a completely different set of jokes. Bob talked about what was funny and what wasn't, illustrating his point with fake noses and portable dog carriers. (The latter was a wire frame with a muzzle on the front and a corkscrew on the back, which, according to Bob, allowed it to be adjusted to fit any size dog.) His performances were sprinkled with non sequiturs.

"I stayed at the Four Seasons Hotel in Chicago. It has a pool on the thirty-fourth floor. Do you have any idea how *deep* that is?"

"I was in the London underground the other day. There's a sign there that reads, 'Dogs must be carried on escalators.' It took me twenty minutes to find one."

"My grandmother always had good advice. She told me, 'Never pet a burning dog,' and 'Don't play leapfrog with a unicorn.'"

"Eight by eight isn't funny; four by sixteen is funny."

If that last sentence stopped you in your tracks, you're not alone.

I learned a valuable lesson in timing from Bob, although he did not teach it to me directly. When Bob performed in front of a large group of people, he would arrange for one person in the audience to be "the holder of the bag." The bag contained two large saucepan lids and a newspaper, which was wrapped around two big, bloody bones. (These were fakes, of course.) At one point, Bob would yell, "Does anybody in the audience have a twelve-inch saucepan lid?" The holder of the bag would yell back, "I do," and would bring the lid down. This would get a big laugh. The gag was repeated with the other lid and the newspaper. Toward the end of the act, Bob would yell, "Does anybody have one of those little drums with the strings with the balls on the ends that goes 'tucka tucka tucka tucka tucka' when you twirl it?" There would be a pause, and the holder of bag would yell back, "What color?"

I told Bob that the next time we were together at a convention and he was going to do the act, I wanted to be the holder of the bag. He said sure; I was delighted. A few years later, I had my chance. But then I started to panic. I knew that all the responses to the various requests for weird items got laughs from the audience, and the "what color" response got a very big laugh. But I wanted that line to get the biggest laugh possible, and the way to do that was to place it at exactly the right time. This is an example of the classic Roadrunner/Coyote situation. Wile E. Coyote has strung a guy wire from the top of a cliff down to a roadway. He's wearing a football helmet with a peg and a grooved wheel on it. The plan is for the Coyote to stand on his head, balancing on the wheel, and then slide down the wire, picking up speed as he goes. When he hits the road he'll have enough speed to catch the Roadrunner. As we watch, realizing that this is one of the stupider plans we've ever seen, the Coyote tries to balance on the wire. He falters, readjusts, almost loses it, and then balances himself perfectly. And at that instant, the wire snaps, and he plunges to the ground below.

I'm obsessed with the timing of the snapping of that wire. It can snap at any time and still be funny. But because of the genius of Chuck Jones and his animators, it snaps at the moment that is *always* funny, no matter how many times you see the cartoon. The timing is perfect. This is what I wanted to do with the "what color" line.

As I sat in the audience with the bag of stuff, I agonized over this. Without trial and error (which I did not have the luxury of), how do you determine the best time to place a punch line? I decided that the way to do it was not to guess, but to make the situation real. So, when Bob asked the question about the drum, I leaned down, opened the bag, looked inside, imagined that I saw several drums of different colors, and then asked, "What color?" By doing so, I found the moment; it got a huge laugh. I made the situation real for me, which made it real for the audience, which made it really funny. Over the years, I had the opportunity to try this approach several more times, and it worked each time.

Bob liked magic tricks that had simple, direct effects: the cups and balls, the knife through coat, the vanish of a glass from under a bowler hat, the wine bottle production. The path to those effects, however, was never direct. It was sprinkled with odd bits of business, gags, one-liners, audience interaction, and even songs. For one routine, Bob provided his own vocal accompaniment, singing *Hong Kong Blues*, an obscure Hoagy Carmichael tune that I have never heard anyone else perform. Bob hated time limits. This is the second reason he wouldn't be effective on TV.

There are a group of magicians that I refer to as "mirror magicians"; their acts are exactly the same whether they are in front of an audience or practicing in front of a mirror. For the most part, stage magicians are in this category, and that's okay, they rarely interact with the audience. Because of their proximity to the spectators, close-up and parlor magicians have a more intimate relationship. I hate to see a close-up magician whose performance excludes the audience. For me, having the audience take the show in an unexpected direction is what makes performing fun. And for Bob Read, it was the whole point. Bob could do his act without the audience interaction, but that would be like a jazz musician playing the melody of a tune without any personal embellishment – why bother? And because Bob loved for the audience to help him discover new, funny bits, whenever he found himself under a time limit, he got flustered.

About twenty-five years ago, Bob competed in a magic contest in Las Vegas. The contest boasted a $5000 first prize. This was a lot of money for the early 1980s, and was an unheard of amount of money for a magic contest. Many fine magicians competed. There was a twelve-minute time limit; if you went over the time limit your score suffered severely. I know that Bob could have done the tricks he had chosen (the wine bottle production, the vanish of a glass under a hat, the cups and balls) in twelve minutes, but as soon as he started, he focused on the time limit instead of the act.

He began to rush; once that happened, the entire rhythm of his performance got thrown off. Bob got through the bottle production without any problems. Then the fun started. The glass vanish is a version of a trick you've probably seen your uncle do with a salt shaker at the dinner table. The shaker is wrapped in a napkin; the napkin is crushed and the shaker vanishes, making its appearance from beneath the table, or from the magician's coat. What made Bob's version great is that he did the trick standing up. He took a normal glass tumbler and wrapped it with a piece of newspaper. He then covered it with his bowler. His next move was to show that the paper-wrapped glass was still on the table. He lifted the bowler, but as he did so, he squeezed the hat, inadvertently grabbing the paper cover. The bowler came up with the glass-shaped piece of newspaper inside it. He lifted the bowler with a flourish, bringing it up over his head, at which time he relaxed his grip slightly, and the piece of newspaper flew over his head, landing a few feet behind him. Bob never saw it go.

Bob was directing his attention to the audience when he threw the paper over his head. He looked down at the glass, and was dumbfounded to see that the piece of newspaper was no longer wrapped around the glass. He looked in the hat; it was empty. He looked around the table – no paper. The only place he didn't look was directly behind him. The thought occurred to him that he hadn't wrapped the glass in the paper in the first place. He checked his pockets for the newspaper – no paper. I don't believe I have ever seen a human being as fooled as Bob Read was right then. The audience was crying. Bob gave up and moved on to his last trick. I don't recall if he ever found out what had happened.

The greatest Bob Read performance I ever saw was at an I.B.M. convention in Quebec City in 1995. This convention was an organizational disaster. The staff of the hotel had gone on strike just before the convention started. The dealer's room (usually an area that serves as a social focal point of a convention) was hidden away in the bowels of the hotel. The stage shows were sub-par, culminating in the flaming train wreck that was a performer named Mundaka. Mundaka had an avant-garde act that was almost immediately hated by the conservative, magic-hobbyist audience. He was booed by the surly French-Canadian magicians. There was a moment, about two-thirds of the way through his act, where Mundaka could have bailed out, saving himself and the audience further embarrassment. But he blithely ignored this moment, and proceeded to crash and burn in a glorious fashion. (As a tribute to his complete lack of performing sense, I've chosen to immortalize Mundaka in a joke in the next chapter.)

Bob was hired to do close-up shows at the convention. There were six close-up magicians, and each magician did six performances on three consecutive days. The audience was situated in six different rooms, and the performers rotated from room to room. Each performer was to do a maximum of twelve minutes in each room. This time limit was important, because if one performer ran long, it screwed up the whole schedule.

Bob, of course, hated having to perform under a time constraint. He did the best he could, but he was extremely dissatisfied with his performances. It became obvious to those of us who knew Bob well that there was an enormous amount of pent-up creative energy waiting to burst free. On the last day of the convention, a crowd of people began to form outside the rooms where the close-up shows were held. I was part of that crowd; we were waiting to see where Bob was going to do his final show, because in that room there would be no time constraints. Once we determined his schedule, everyone piled into that final room. The room was packed to overflowing; had a fire marshal walked in – well, he couldn't have walked in; there wasn't any place left to stand.

We had all assumed that Bob would be in rare form in that final room; we had no idea just how great he would be. When he walked into the room and saw that it was packed to overflowing, a huge smile spread over his face. This is how he liked to work, with the crowd right on top of him. He invited a man to sit at a table in the front of the room. And then, he let loose. He did five minutes with a squeaky door. He showed us how the Invisible Man does karate. He riffed on a woman who couldn't stop giggling. He worked for an hour and five minutes, and he hadn't done a single trick.

He did five more minutes as he brought out a deck of cards. He took the cards from the case, handed them to the man sitting at the table, and asked him to shuffle them. The man, who was still shaking with laughter, panicked, and as he tried to shuffle the cards he shot them all over the floor.

Bob looked at him, horrified. "Jesus Christ!" he said. "What the fuck are you doing? I've only got twelve minutes!" Pandemonium.

Before we left Bob and Pauline in October of 2005 I signed their guestbook. I had signed it ten years earlier. That my signature was in this book was a bit of a surprise to Bob and me. Bob had forgotten that I had stayed with them. I remembered that I had stayed, but I had no memory of why I had been in England. That, unfortunately, was a period of my life when I forgot more than I remembered. Bob and Pauline promised to visit us in Vegas after the history conference.

The following month Bob gave his talk in Los Angeles. As expected, he had worked out some funny bits utilizing the PowerPoint technology. After the conference, he and Pauline vacationed in California. While there, he suffered a massive heart attack and died in his hotel room.

I learned of Bob's death via the Internet. It hit me hard. With Dad,

Jay, and Billy, I had a deep sense of sadness and loss, but this was tempered by the knowledge of inevitability. This is how life works – people grow old; people die. With Bob all I had was a feeling of selfish outrage; I just could not accept the fact that this man would no longer be around to make me laugh. But you can't treat life the way some magicians treat their audiences – as if you're sitting behind a mirror. Anytime you do that, life, like some wisecracking spectator, is going to toss you something you're not prepared to handle. And Bob's death was very hard to handle.

I wanted to write something about Bob right after he died, and I found that I couldn't. Words didn't seem adequate. Even now, almost two years after his death, I feel like I'm playing that game where you have to describe a spiral without using your hands. If you ever saw him perform, you know what I mean. If you never saw him, well, I just wish that you had.

I think of Bob often; most of these thoughts are jumbled memories of laughter, and craziness, and comments that initially make no sense but pay off forty minutes later. If I close my eyes, I can see him in the middle of his manic knife through coat routine. He has plunged a large knife blade through the jacket of a hapless spectator. As he attempts to mend the hole, Bob apparently starts pulling out the lining of the spectator's coat. A bit of cloth comes out, and then the entire lining comes out in a long, narrow strip. The audience falls over with laughter. Many years ago, when he first began doing the trick, Bob had used an eight by eight, square piece of cloth as the fake lining. But it just wasn't funny.

James B.

I saw the movie *Goldfinger* when I was twelve years old. I loved it. My Uncle Jack was in the Army Reserve, and, for a few weeks, was stationed at Fort Knox during the time the movie was in theaters. We visited him, and it was a thrill to see the actual locations used in the movie. My cousins and I played "Bond vs. Odd Job" with a Frisbee. Because I was a kid who loved books, I really wanted to read the Ian Fleming novels. I bought a paperback copy of the book *Goldfinger* when I was thirteen. My Mom was not so sure that the book was appropriate for someone my age, so she read through it first. She found everything to be suitable, except for the last dozen or so pages. Rather than completely ban the book, she simply stapled those pages together. Obedient son that I was, I never tried to take the staples out.

I mention this story for two reasons. (Three, if you include confirmation that when I was a kid I was an idiot.) First, we have come to the chapter with the really dirty jokes. If such jokes are reprehensible and objectionable to you, grab a stapler and staple together pages 175 through 206. That way you won't be exposed to material that could warp your young, impressionable mind. But before you do that, let's be honest with each other. There have been some fairly raunchy jokes in the previous chapters, and the ones that are coming up are not really that much worse. If your head hasn't exploded up to this point, you'll probably be fine when you reach the end of this chapter. Also, just to be perverse, I've dropped some clean jokes into this chapter, so if you staple it shut, you'll miss out on those. And I know that in your heart you're dying to read these jokes, so just who are we kidding here?

The second reason I mention the James Bond story is that I'd really like to know how *Goldfinger* ends, so if you know, drop me a line.

There is no real organization to this chapter. Most of the jokes came to mind as I was writing other chapters, and I just saved them for this section.

One of the big problems with a really dirty joke is loosening up the crowd, putting them in the mood for raunchy material. Sometimes you'll be telling jokes to people, and you'll think they're ready for a good dirty joke, but you're not sure. The following bit of business will help break the ice.

> I want to tell all of you a joke, but it's a little off color. There's a word in the joke that I'm not really comfortable using, since I don't know you that well. So if I say "make love," you'll know what word I would normally use, right? Is everybody okay with that? Fine, here's the joke. These two cocksuckers are walking down the street...

Now that we have that out of the way, here are some jokes.

> A man in Chicago is reading the want ads in an alternative newspaper. One ad catches his eye: "Wanted – Pubic Hair Stylist." There is a New York City phone number at the bottom of the ad, and, intrigued, the man dials it. A man answers the phone, and the fellow in Chicago says, "I saw your ad in a paper here in Chicago. What's the job all about?"
>
> "It's really pretty simple," says the man in New York. "You'll be working with performers in the adult film industry, styling, trimming, shaving, and shaping the pubic hair of some of the most beautiful women in the world. You work Tuesday through Thursday, 10 a.m. to 2 p.m. The job pays $200,000 a year, plus full medical and dental benefits."
>
> "To be honest," says the man in Chicago, "I really don't have any experience in this area." "Not a problem," says the other man. "We'll teach you everything you need to know."
>
> "In that case, I'm very interested in this job. Could I come for an interview?" "Absolutely," says the man in New York. "Can you be in Philadelphia on Tuesday?"

"Yes, I can, but I thought the job is in New York."

"It is, but the *line*..."

*

A little Jewish accountant is convicted of embezzlement. Due to a clerical mix up, he is sent to a maximum security prison and is assigned to a cell with an enormous black man. The black man looks up from his cot as the accountant enters the cell.

"Well, looky here," he says. "I've got me a new roommate. Roomie, you and me are going to play 'husband and wife.' Do you want to be the husband or do you want to be the wife?" The accountant considers this for a moment. "I think I'll be the husband," he replies.

Puzzled, the black man thinks about this. Then he says, "All right then. Husband, come over here and suck your wife's dick."

*

Two convicts are given a chance at early parole. They are to go out into the public school system, give talks with an anti-drug message, and get the students to sign a pledge that they won't do drugs. Whoever can get the most signatures wins an early parole.

The men give their motivational speeches for two weeks. By the end of that time, the first convict has accumulated two thousand signatures. The warden says, "That's very impressive. How did you convince so many students?" "It was really pretty easy," says the convict. "I drew two circles on the blackboard; one circle was large, the other was very small. I pointed to the large circle and said, 'This is your brain.' Then I pointed to the other circle and I said, 'This is your brain on drugs.'"

The other convict comes in. He has accumulated twenty thousand signatures. The warden is overwhelmed. "How in the world did you manage to sway so many students?" he asks. "It was pretty easy," says the second convict. "I drew two circles on the blackboard; one circle was very small, the other was very large. I pointed to the small circle and said, 'This is your asshole before prison...'"

*

It's two o'clock in the morning, and two very drunk leprechauns are pounding on the door of a convent. The mother superior opens the door. "Aye, we're real sorry to be bothering you so early in the mornin'," says one of them, "but do you have any really short nuns here?"

"Well, Sister Teresa is a very short woman; she's about four foot ten." "Oh, no, no, no," says the leprechaun, "I'm talkin' eye-to-eye with me; two feet tall tops."

"No," says the mother superior, "there's no one here that small."

The first leprechaun punches the second one in the shoulder. "You see, Sean; I told you that you were fuckin' a penguin!"

*

Two nuns are driving through Transylvania. Suddenly, a vampire lands on the hood of their car. He presses his face against the windshield. The younger nun says, "What should we do; what should we do?" The older nun says, "Show him your cross."

The younger nun sticks her head out the window and yells, "Hey asshole! Get the fuck off our car!"

*

A college professor is giving a lecture to a class in human sexuality. "Not counting mirror images and bilateral reflections, there are seventy-three possible sexual positions for a man and a woman." A man in the front row raises his hand. "I'm sorry to disagree, Professor, but there are seventy-four." "I assure you, young man, that there are only seventy-three." "And I assure you, Professor, that back home in France I have personally experienced seventy-four different positions."

"Well," says the professor, "I guess the only way to settle this is to enumerate each position. Let's start with the basic Missionary Position – the woman lies on her back with her legs apart; the man lies on top of the woman, facing her."

The Frenchman shouts, "Oh, my God, seventy-five!"

*

A professor is giving a lecture in human sexuality. "Before we start," he says, "let's take an informal survey. How many of you have sex more than twice a week?" A few hands go up. "How many of you have sex at least once a week?" A few more hands are raised. "How many of you have sex twice a month?" This seems to be a popular frequency, and many hands go up. "How many of you have sex once a month?" A few hands are raised.

By this time, the professor notices that one man has not raised his hand. "Every other month?" The man shakes his head. "Three times a year?" The man shakes his head no. "Twice a year?" Again, no. "Once a year?" The man cracks a big smile and enthusiastically waves his hand in the air. "Are you telling me that you only have sex once a year?" The man shakes his head yes. "Then why are you smiling?"

The man says, "Tonight's the night!"

*

A wealthy man decides to leave the rat race. He buys some land in the Ozarks, bulldozes off the top of a small mountain, and builds a beautiful estate. It has a satellite/cable hookup, and a helipad for the monthly delivery of supplies.

The man lives there for several months, and realizes that he's getting a little lonely. One day, there's a knock on his door. He opens it and discovers a big, burly, mountain man standing on his front porch. "Howdy neighbor," says the mountain man. "I'm your neighbor. I live on the top of that mountain over there. I noticed the helicopter flying off the other day, and I thought to myself, 'Hey, I've got a neighbor.' So, I thought I'd come over and say howdy and invite you to a little welcoming party."

"A party? Really? That's great," says the man. "Yeah, it's going to be a whole lot of fun. There's going to be drinking, and food, and fighting, and fucking, and more drinking, and more food, and more fighting, and more fucking."

"That sounds great," says the man. "How shall I dress?"

"Don't matter," says the mountain man, "it's just going to be you and me."

*

An old woman goes to the supermarket. She buys some bread, a few tomatoes, and some shredded cheese. She calls one of the stock boys over. "Jimmy," she says, "where's the butter?" "I'm sorry, Mrs. Jones," says the stock boy. "We're out of butter until tomorrow."

The woman buys some canned soup, some crackers, and some cream. She waves for Jimmy to come over. "Jimmy," she says, "where's the butter?" "I'm sorry, Mrs. Jones," says the stock boy. "We're out of butter. We won't get another delivery of butter until tomorrow morning."

The woman buys some cat food, some tissues, and some sherbet. She waves for Jimmy to come over. "Jimmy," she says, "where's the butter?" "Mrs. Jones, you were a school teacher, weren't you?" asks Jimmy. "That's right," says Mrs. Jones. "In that case, ma'am, how do spell 'cat' as in catsup?" "C-A-T." "And how do you spell 'dog' as in dog food?" "D-O-G." "And how do you spell 'fuck' as in butter?" "Why Jimmy, there's no 'fuck' in butter," says Mrs. Jones.

"That's what I've been trying to tell you for the last ten minutes!"

*

Jimmy the stock boy is working in the produce department when a big Texan walks up to him. "I'd like a half a head of lettuce, please," says the Texan. "Excuse me?" says Jimmy. "I'd like a half a head of lettuce, please," the Texan says again. "Just a minute," says Jimmy. He walks to the front of the store, where the manager is standing. Unbeknownst to Jimmy, the Texan has followed him.

"You're not going to believe this," says Jimmy to the manager. "Some dumbass wants to buy a half a head of lettuce." Jimmy turns and sees that the Texan is standing right behind him. "And this fine gentleman would like to buy the other half."

[When I tell this, I do a Texas drawl for the voice of the Texan. Jimmy's last line is also done in a Texas drawl.]

*

The manager is impressed with the way Jimmy handled the Texan. "That was some pretty quick thinking back there," he says. "I'd like to make you the manager of my store in Toronto." "Why the hell would I want to move to Canada?" says Jimmy. "The only people there are hookers and hockey players." "Really?" says the manager. "My wife is Canadian."

"Is she?" says Jimmy. "What team does she play for?"

*

Jimmy the stock boy is cashiering at the grocery store. A woman comes to check out her groceries. She has two small children with her. "Are those two twins?" asks Jimmy. "Why no," says the woman. "One is four and the other is six. Why did you think they were twins?"

"I just couldn't believe that someone would fuck you twice."

*

Jimmy the stock boy is cashiering at the grocery store. A woman comes to check out her groceries. She's purchasing a pork chop, a pound of ground beef, one baking potato, three TV dinners, two muffins, and a small container of milk. Jimmy rings up all these items and says to her, "You're single, aren't you." "Yes, I am," says the woman. "What tipped you off, my food items?"

"No, you're just fucking ugly."

*

A man takes a cruise and discovers that Brooke Shields is also on the ship. By an unfortunate turn of events, the ship sinks, and the man and Brooke Shields are washed up on the beach of a deserted island; they are the only survivors. The man is resourceful; he builds two small shelters, and he finds fresh water and fruit. He learns to fish, and he hunts small animals for meals.

After a month, Brooke has become quite fond of the man. One night she goes to his shelter, climbs into his bed, and they make passionate love. The next night, after dinner, the man timidly approaches her. "I was wondering if you would do something for me," he says. "Sure," says Brooke. "Would you put on these clothes?" he asks, handing her some men's clothing. "Okay," she says. "And would you tuck your hair up under this?" he says, handing her a man's hat. "Okay," she says. "And can I put a small moustache on you?" "Okay," she says, and he uses some of the ash from the fire to draw a moustache on her. "And can I call you Frank?" he asks. "Okay," she says.

The man walks up to her, looks around, and says, "Frank, you're not going to believe who I fucked last night!"

Looking over the previous chapters of this book, I realized that I had not included any golf jokes. I'm putting all of them here. I don't play golf, but when I worked at Illusions many of the magicians learned to play so they could hang with the guy who owned the place. I used that bit of information as my lead in, and told many of the following jokes in my stand-up magic act.

> A man retires as a senior executive for a real estate development company. He says to his wife, "Listen, we have a lot of free time now. You know how much I love to play golf; I'd like to play golf with you. Why don't you let me sign you up for some lessons with the golf pro at the country club? Then we could play together." The wife agrees, and the next day she has her first lesson with the club pro.
>
> The lesson is a disaster. The woman can't even understand how to grip a golf club. The pro has reached the end of his patience. "Listen, Mrs. Jones," he tells the woman, "the problem is that you are visualizing the golf club as some type of foreign object. That's why you can't get comfortable with it. Let me try something. You're a woman of the world, so let's try this: Don't think of this as a golf club; imagine that it's your husband's penis."
>
> Wham! The golf ball goes three hundred yards, straight down the fairway. The pro says, "That was very good. Now take the club out of your mouth..."

*

> A man decides that learning to play golf will enhance his networking abilities. He buys a medium-priced set of clubs, a decent pair of shoes, a few inexpensive golf balls, and heads out to a public golf course. He tees up his first ball, arranges his stance, and slices the ball way out into the rough on the right side of the fairway. His first impulse is to tee up another ball, but he then decides that golf balls aren't cheap, so he walks into the rough to find the missing ball.
>
> As he's searching for his ball, he finds another golf ball that someone has lost in the rough. Concluding that he will probably lose a lot of golf balls during his practice

sessions, the man pockets the ball. He continues to search for his golf ball, and, by the time he finds it, he has found and pocketed a dozen other lost golf balls.

He walks out of the rough, and sees a woman who is about to take a shot from the fairway. The woman looks over at the man and stares intently at the very large bulge in his pocket. Embarrassed, the man looks down at the bulge. "Golf balls," he says to the woman.

She replies, "Is that anything like tennis elbow?"

*

Tiger Woods is playing a round of golf at the Augusta National Golf Club. On his second shot on the tenth hole, he hooks the ball way off to the left. He walks over to find it, and discovers that his ball is resting in a patch of buttercups. He takes out a wedge and prepares to hit the ball out of the flowers when suddenly, in a flash of light, Mother Nature appears.

"Please don't hit that ball," says Mother Nature. "If you hit the ball you'll destroy many of the flowers, and buttercups are my personal favorites. If you spare the flowers, I will provide you with all the butter you could ever want for the rest of your life."

Tiger Woods says, "Where the hell were you back on the eighth when I was in the pussy willows?"

*

A man is talking to some colleagues at work on Monday morning. He takes an orange golf ball out of his pocket. "Check this out," he says. "This is the greatest idea since the invention of the game of golf. This is a golf ball that you can never lose. It's day-glow orange, so you see it easily on the fairway. If you listen, you can hear it beeping. You can track it down even if you hit it in the rough. If you hit it into a water trap, there's a pocket of air inside it, and the ball floats to the surface. The dimples on the outside expand and contract, so the ball automatically works its way back to solid ground."

"Well, that's pretty amazing," says one of the men. "Where did you get it?"

"I found it."

*

Four friends are playing golf at their country club one weekend. The foursome ahead of them is lagging, and this is beginning to piss off the men. By the time they reach the back nine, they are openly taking shots at the four men ahead of them. As the men finish the 18th hole, the golf pro of the country club walks up to them. "Listen," he says, "I saw what you guys were doing back there, and I know you think you're pretty cute. But what you don't know is that the four men ahead of you are blind; they play with golf balls that give off a small radio signal. That's why they were playing so slowly."

One of the men says, "Wow, I am really sorry. Please go inside and tell them that the next time they play their green fees are on me."

The second man says, "If they're having lunch here, please tell them that their meals are on me."

The third man says, "And tell them to go to the bar and have whatever they want. Their drinks are on me.

The fourth man says, "Fuck 'em. Tell 'em to play at night."

*

Four men who work in the same company play golf every Saturday. One of the foursome is transferred to another city. When his replacement comes to work, one of the men asks him if he plays golf. "Yes, I do," the man replies. "We play at the public course every Saturday at 8 a.m. Will you join us?" "Sure," says the man. "But I might be twenty minutes late."

On Saturday morning the four men arrive at the golf course. The newest member of the foursome tees up. He's left handed; he has a beautiful swing and he drives the ball with a remarkable amount of power. The ball goes two hundred yards straight down the fairway. At the end of the round, he has soundly beaten the other three men.

"You're an amazing golfer," says one man. "I've learned a lot just watching you play. Will you play with us again next Saturday, same time, 8 a.m.?" "I'd be glad to," says the man. "But I might be twenty minutes late."

The next Saturday, the men arrive at 8 a.m. This time, the newcomer has a set of right-handed clubs. He drives with even more power than he did the week before. The ball goes two hundred fifty yards down the fairway. He proceeds to beat the other three more soundly than he did previously.

"Wow," says one man. "That was remarkable. It's obvious that you're comfortable playing right handed or left handed. How do you decide which way to play?" "I leave it up to my wife. When I wake up, if she's sleeping on her right side I play right handed; if she's sleeping on her left side I play left handed." "What if she's sleeping on her back?"

"I'm twenty minutes late."

*

Two men are playing golf at their country club. Two women are playing ahead of them, and they are lagging severely. One man says to the other, "I'm going to walk up there and ask them if we can play through."

The man jogs up the fairway toward the women. Suddenly, he stops, turns around, and jogs back. "I can't talk to them," he says. "One of the women is my wife, and the other is this gal I've been banging on the side." "I'll go talk to them," says the other man.

He jogs toward the women, stops when he is fifty feet away, and jogs back. He says, "Small world, isn't it?"

*

> God and Moses are playing golf. Moses hits his first tee shot. It goes two hundred yards straight down the fairway. God hits his first tee shot. It hooks off to the left into a water trap. Before the ball can sink out of sight, the water parts, leaving ball resting on the muddy bottom of the pond. A squirrel races across the bottom of the pond, picks up the ball in his mouth, and runs back out onto the fairway. An eagle swoops down from above and grabs the squirrel in his talons. The eagle takes off into the air. A lightning bolt shoots out of the sky and strikes the eagle. The eagle drops the squirrel, which hits the green. The ball pops out of the squirrel's mouth, rolls six feet, and drops into the cup for a hole in one.
>
> Moses turns to God and says, "So, are we going to play golf, or are you going to fuck around?"

Penn Jillette's wife Emily is an avid golfer. When I told her I was working on a joke book, she told me two really good golf jokes that I had not heard before.

> A young man, his father, and his grandfather all work for the same company. They play golf in a foursome with another man from the company. That man gets transferred, leaving them short for their golf game. The father's secretary hears them bemoaning the loss of their friend. She asks if she can join them when they play again the next weekend. The men talk it over and decide that even though she's probably a lousy golfer, she's easy on the eyes, so they say yes.
>
> That weekend the secretary joins the three men at the country club. It turns out that she is an excellent golfer, who plays the country club course several times a week. They get to the 18th green. The secretary has a six-foot putt. She says, "If I sink this putt, I'll break my own record for this course. This is very important to me, so I'd like a little advice. I'll have sex with whoever gives me the suggestion that let's me beat my record."
>
> The young man kneels down and eyeballs the putt.

"This green breaks slightly to the right. You'll want to aim about one cup width to the left and putt firmly."

The father kneels down and examines the green. "No, that's not right. This green breaks strongly to the left. You'll want to aim about two cup widths to the right and putt gently."

The grandfather looks at the putt, looks at the secretary, and says, "That's a gimme."

*

The police are called to the scene of a grisly domestic murder. A woman has bludgeoned her husband to death with a seven iron. The bedroom is a gory mess. A policeman says to the wife, "How many times did you hit him?"

"I don't know," says the wife. "Four, five, six times...Put me down for five."

Here are four sick jokes that have a little bite to them. That's why I placed them here.

A man gets a call from the emergency room of a hospital; his wife has been in a very serious car accident. He drives to the hospital and sits in the waiting room outside the intensive care unit. After a few hours a doctor comes out and walks over to him.

"Your wife has suffered extensive head injuries. She's in a coma right now, and, judging from the patterns of her brain activity, I don't believe that she will ever come out of this coma. Unfortunately, your HMO does not cover this type of treatment, and you'll have to move her somewhere else tomorrow. A private care facility will run you hundreds of dollars a day, so you might consider caring for her at home.

"She will be unable to care for herself, so you'll have to feed her and clean her, as well as tending to her every need. You will have to purchase special equipment, so you should consider selling your house, moving into a mobile home, and using the money you make to purchase the supplies you will need.

"I'm guessing that she will stay in this vegetative state for another thirty years, she will require your constant attention for that entire time, and her condition will bury you in debt."

By now, the man is sobbing into his hands.

The doctor pats him on the shoulder. "Hey," he says, "I'm just fucking with you. She's dead."

*

A man answers a knock on his front door. It's the Western Union delivery man, in full uniform. "I have a telegram for you, sir," he says. "This is great," says the man. "Is it a singing telegram? I've never had a singing telegram." "No sir," replies the delivery man, "it's not a singing telegram."

"Would you sing it to me anyway? I would love to have a telegram sung to me. It would be a big thrill." "I couldn't sir, it wouldn't be right." "Please? Pretty please? This would really mean a lot to me."

"Well, all right then." The delivery man clears his throat. "Dah, dah, dah, dah, dah, dah – Your sister Rose is dead."

[The last line is done in your best Broadway style. Be sure to use jazz hands.]

*

An Army private is assigned as a chaplain's assistant. His first duty is to inform Private Smith that his mother has died. The assistant goes into Smith's barracks, walks up to Smith, and says, "Private Smith, your mother's dead." Smith passes out from the shock.

Word of this gets back to the chaplain, who calls his assistant into his office. "That was absolutely the wrong way to break the news to Private Smith," he says. "You need to use tact; you need to break the news gently. I've just heard that Private Jones' mother has died. Try it again, and don't be so blunt this time."

The chaplain's assistant goes to Jones' barracks. He asks all the soldiers to come outside and stand in a line, single file. Addressing the group, he says, "Okay, I want all the men whose mothers are alive to take one step forward. Not so fast, Jones."

*

A young man volunteers to help the United Way campaign in his town. In looking over the donation records, the young man notices that the town's richest and most successful businessman has never donated to the United Way. He pays the businessman a visit at his office.

"We've done some research," says the young man, "and we noticed that even though you have several businesses and properties that are worth many millions of dollars, you have never donated any money to the United Way."

"Really," says the businessman. "Did your research show that my mother is dying after a long, painful illness, and that she has incurred huge medical bills far beyond her ability to pay?" "No, we weren't aware of that," says the young man.

"And did you know that my brother, a disabled veteran of the Gulf War, is blind, confined to a wheelchair, and unable to support his wife and five children?" "No, we didn't know that," says the young man.

"And did you know that my sister's husband died in a horrible car accident, leaving her penniless with four children and a large mortgage?" "No, we weren't...we didn't..."

"And if I don't give anything to *them*, why the fuck should I give anything to *you*?"

In this book you've encountered jokes that have the same basic set-up, but that have different punch lines. Here are two more pairs.

> A male and a female astronaut are sent deep into outer space. They land on a planet inhabited by sen-

tient robots. The astronauts and the robot leaders are exchanging information when the subject of reproduction comes up. The astronauts express interest in seeing how the robots procreate.

A male and a female robot intertwine tentacles. They quiver for a few moments, the female's stomach area turns red, a small hatch opens, and a baby robot pops out.

The robots ask the astronauts to demonstrate human reproduction. The two are embarrassed, but they feel that it is necessary for the sake of science. They undress, lie down on the floor, and make love. When they finish, they see that the robots are laughing hysterically. "What's so funny about that?" asks the male astronaut.

"That's how we make cars!"

*

[Follow the previous joke up to the point where the astronauts make love. Then continue thusly:]

When they finish, they see that the robots are looking at them quizzically. "Where is the baby?" one of them asks. "Well, the baby, if there is a baby, and there's no guarantee that there will be one, will be born nine months from now."

"Nine months?" asks the robot. "That's right," says the astronaut.

"Then why the big hurry at the end?"

*

A man joins a group of cowboys who are herding several hundred sheep across the plains of Montana. They have been out on the range for several weeks, and the man is feeling the pangs of sexual frustration. He approaches one of the other men. "What do you guys do when you get really horny?" asks the man. "Well, we usually just do it to one of the sheep," the cowboy replies. The man is initially repulsed by the idea, but as the weeks go by, and he gets hornier and hornier, the thought of sex with a sheep seems less horrible.

One night, he just can't stand it any more. He sneaks into the herd, finds a sheep, and screws it. When he finishes, he hears laughter, and as his eyes adjust to the darkness he sees that all the other cowboys are standing around watching him. "Hey, you said that you all do the same thing," he says to them. "Why are you laughing at me?"

"Because you fucked an ugly one!"

*

[Follow the joke above up to the point where the guy has sex with the sheep. Then proceed as follows.]

When the man finishes, he looks around and sees that the other cowboys are watching him with horrified looks on their faces. "What are you looking at me like that for?" asks the man. "You all do the same thing."

"Yeah," says one of the cowboys, "but you fucked Big Jake's girl!"

And that reminds me.

In the 1800s, a man heads out to the Black Hills of South Dakota to do some prospecting. He spends many weeks out in the wild, panning for gold. After a month or so, he feels the need for human companionship, so he rides to a small town. He walks into the only saloon in town, orders a drink, and starts to talk to the bartender. "Tell me, barkeep," he says. "Where could a fellow find some female company in this town?" "There are no women in this town, stranger," says the bartender. "No women?" says the man. "What do you do when you get horny?" "Fortunately," says the bartender, "we have old Charlie." "You have sex with old Charlie?" asks the man. "That's right," says the bartender.

"No way," says the man. He finishes his drink and

heads back out to his prospecting camp. A few more weeks go by, and his sexual frustration grows worse. He rides back into town, goes back into the saloon, and speaks to the bartender. "Listen, if I have sex with old Charlie, who would know about it?" "Well," says the bartender, "I'd have to set it up, so I'd know about it. Obviously, you'd know about it. Old Charlie would know about it. And then there'd be Jake, Luke, Steve, and Bert."

"Jake, Luke, Steve, and Bert? Who the hell are they?" asks the man.

"They hold down old Charlie. See, he doesn't care for this, either."

[My normal phrasing for the punch line of this joke is "he don't dig this either," which is a phrase that citizens of the 1800s wouldn't use. When you tell the joke, that glitch slides by; in print, it sticks out like a sore thumb. I just didn't want any smartass to write me and correct my jargon.]

*

A man joins the French Foreign Legion. He is stationed at a fort in the middle of the desert. After several months, pangs of sexual yearning spring up. The man goes to the sergeant of the fort. "What do the men here do for sexual release?" he asks. "We usually use one of the camels," says the sergeant. The man is somewhat revolted by the idea, and he goes back to his barracks to take a cold shower.

More months pass; the man can't stand it anymore. In the middle of the night he sets a ladder behind a camel, climbs up, and has sex with it. As he is climbing down the ladder he sees the sergeant and the other soldiers laughing at him. He says to the sergeant, "You told me that when they get horny the men use a camel."

"That's right," says the sergeant. "But we throw a saddle on it and ride to town."

*

At the beginning of the Iraqi War, an Army ambulance is driving down a road on the outskirts of Baghdad. The driver of the ambulance sees two bodies lying in the road; one is an Iraqi soldier, the other is a U.S. soldier. Both men are badly injured. The Iraqi is unconscious; the soldiers put him in the back of the ambulance. The American soldier can speak. "What happened here?" asks the ambulance driver.

"I was patrolling this road alone," says the soldier, "when I saw an Iraqi soldier approaching me. We stopped when we were about twenty feet apart. I yelled, 'Fuck Saddam Hussein!' He yelled, 'Fuck George Bush!' And while we were hugging we got hit by a truck."

*

A little boy is in the men's restroom in Grand Central Station. He sees a sailor washing his hands. "Gosh," says the little boy, "are you a real sailor?" "Yes, I am," says the sailor. "Would you like to wear my hat for a few minutes?" "Gosh, yes. Thanks a lot." The little boy puts on the sailor hat.

The boy wanders around the restroom; he sees a marine stepping away from a urinal. "Gosh," says the little boy, "are you a real marine?" "Yes, I am," says the marine. "Would you like to suck my dick?"

"Oh, I'm not a real sailor. I'm just wearing his hat."

*

A soldier has been taking paratrooper training. Today is the day of his first jump from an airplane and he is very nervous about it. "I'm just not sure that I can step out of the plane," he tells the soldier in the bunk above him. "You'll be fine," the soldier says. "You've had excellent training, and you know exactly what to do. Just double check your equipment, mentally run through all the things you're supposed to do, and keep your wits about you. You'll be fine."

The soldier leaves; he returns several hours later. "How did it go?" asks his friend. "Well, I was okay for a while, but as I got closer and closer to the door I got more and more afraid. When I reached the door, I just couldn't go out. I froze. I couldn't move. The big black drill sergeant said to me, 'Boy, if you don't get yourself out of this airplane, I'm going to shove my dick up your ass!'"

"Wow, did you jump?" asks the friend.

"A little, at first."

*

A gay man is infatuated with a proctologist who lives in his apartment building. In an effort to meet the doctor, the man makes an appointment at his clinic. He sits in the examination room, waiting for the doctor. The doctor comes in. "What seems to be the problem?" he asks.

"It hurts back there," says the man. The doctor has the man drop his pants and bend over the examination table. He reaches up the man's ass and pulls out a long-stemmed red rose.

"Holy smoke," the doctor says, "you had a long-stemmed, red rose up your ass."

The man says, "Read the note; read the note!"

Let's change the subject.

A missionary has been assigned to a remote African village. As he walks around the village with the chief, he takes the opportunity to expand the chief's English vocabulary. The missionary points to the cooking fire in the center of the village. "This is a fire. In English we call this 'fire'," he says. They come to a large tree. "This is a tree. In English we call this 'tree'." They walk toward the edge of the village. The missionary points to some bushes. "These are bushes. In English the word is 'bushes'."

Just then, the bushes move as the result of some energetic activity within them. The chief and the missionary see a couple making passionate love behind the bushes. "What that called?" asks the chief. Wanting to sidestep an uncomfortable discussion, the missionary says, "We call that 'riding a bicycle'." The chief whips out a blow gun and shoots two poison darts into the couple, killing them instantly. "Why in the world did you do that?" asks the missionary.

"He riding *my* bicycle."

*

A missionary is sent to Africa; his job is to bring the word of God to a remote village. When the missionary arrives at the village, he asks the chief to have everyone assemble around him. "I'm here from the United States of America to bring you the teachings of Jesus Christ," says the minister. The crowd of villagers yells, "Mundaka! Mundaka!" "Through His teachings I will show you the way to eternal salvation," says the minister. The crowd responds, "Mundaka! Mundaka!" "And you will no longer be savages; your lives will have dignity and meaning. I will help you replace your primitive beliefs with the true word of God!" says the minister. "Mundaka! Mundaka! Mundaka!" yells the crowd, jumping up and down enthusiastically.

The minister is overwhelmed by the emotional response of the villagers. When he regains his composure, he asks the chief for a tour of the village. The chief shows him around, eventually coming to a pasture where several large bulls are grazing. "May I take a closer look at those bulls?" asks the minister. "Sure," says the chief. "Just be careful that you don't step in the mundaka."

*

An Englishman, a Frenchman, and a Pole have been captured by cannibals. The chief says, "We are going to kill you, dine on your entrails, and use your skin to make our canoes. Do you have a last request?" The Englishman says, "Give me a knife." The cannibals give the Englishman a knife. He says, "God save the Queen," and slits his own throat. The Frenchman says, "Give me a knife." The cannibals give the Frenchman a knife. He says, "Viva la France," and slits his own throat. The Pole says, "Give me a fork." The cannibals give him a fork. He jabs the fork all over his body and yells, "There goes your fucking canoe!"

*

The doorbell rings at a whorehouse. The madam opens the door. Standing on the front stoop is a man who is in a full-body cast. His head is covered with bandages. The madam asks, "What the hell do you want?" "I want sex," says the man. "Look at you," the madam replies. "You can't do anything."

The man says, "Hey, I rang the doorbell, didn't I?"

*

A man walks into a barber shop on a Thursday afternoon. "How many ahead of me?" he asks. "Three," says the barber. "Great," says the man, and he leaves. On Friday afternoon he comes in again. "How many ahead of me?" he asks. "Four," says the barber. "Outstanding," says the man, and he leaves. He comes in again on Saturday afternoon. The barber shop is hopping. "How many ahead of me?" asks the man. "Six," says the barber. "Terrific," says the man, and he leaves.

This time, the barber's curiosity overwhelms him. "Jim," he says to one of the men in the shop, "follow that guy and tell me where he goes." Jim leaves the shop. He comes back a few minutes later. "Where did he go?" asks the barber.

"Your house."

*

Four friends head out to the woods to do some hunting. They draw straws to see who will do the cooking. Whoever gets the short straw cooks, and he must continue to cook until someone complains about the food. Whoever complains has to take over the cooking chores. Frank gets the short straw, and he cooks dinner the first night.

The hunting trip continues; no one complains about the food, and Frank is stuck preparing the meals. He's fed up with it. So, one afternoon, while his buddies are out looking for animals to shoot, he gathers up a bowl of moose droppings, and he stirs them into the stew he is preparing.

The hunters come back to camp and sit down for dinner. Frank spoons out healthy portions of the stew to each of them. One of the men digs out a big spoonful of stew and pops it in his mouth. He immediately spits it out. "Jesus H. Christ," he yells, "this tastes like moose shit...but good!"

The next joke is a great one to tell to anyone who's old enough to remember the key players of the Nixon administration. If your spectator answers perfectly, here's the way the joke goes.

Me: Apparently, the last few weeks of the Nixon administration were completely out of control. I heard a story that Nixon was showing Gerald and Betty Ford around the White house, explaining some of the things they'd need to know when they moved in. Anyway, Nixon opens the door of the Lincoln bedroom, and it was unbelievable. There on the bed is Pat Nixon and Henry...what's his name...the Secretary of State..."

My friend: Kissinger?

Me: No! Fucking 'er!

Some years ago, a contest was held on the Internet to choose the world's funniest joke. (I think there might have been a stipulation that it had to be a clean joke.) I was familiar with the joke that won; I had been telling it for years. Here it is.

Sherlock Holmes and his faithful companion Dr. Watson go on a camping trip. They set up their tent, cook dinner, smoke after-dinner cigars, and turn in for the

> night. Around one in morning, Holmes wakes up Watson. "Watson, look up at the sky and tell me what you see."
>
> "I see millions of stars, Holmes." "And from this observation, what can you deduce?"
>
> Watson thinks about this for a moment. "In terms of astronomy, I can deduce that there are millions of galaxies and potentially billions of planets, many of which might support life. If I believed in astrology, I would know that Saturn is in Leo. In terms of time of day, I can tell that it is a little past one in the morning. Theologically, it is evident that the Lord is powerful and all-encompassing and we are small and insignificant. Meteorologically, I can make an educated guess that we will have a clear, beautiful day tomorrow. Why, Holmes, what do the stars tell you?"
>
> "You idiot, they tell me that some son-of-a-bitch stole our tent!"

This is certainly a clever and humorous joke, but in no way is it the funniest joke in the world (clean or dirty). The joke simply serves as a reminder that anything posted on the Internet has to be taken with a huge grain of salt.

To end this chapter, I offer you a series of jokes, each of which is funnier than the Holmes/Watson joke. The final joke may well be the best joke I've ever told.

> A man is walking through Japan. He comes to a small village, where he sees a small man dressed in bronze Samurai garments. He has a long sword and a small box attached to his sash. "Who are you?" asks the man. "I am the third greatest Samurai warrior in all of Japan. Would you like a demonstration?" The bronze warrior opens the top of the box attached to his sash. A fly buzzes out. The fly flits around the warrior's head. He swiftly draws his sword and swings it at the fly. The fly is neatly sliced in half and drops to the ground. The man compliments the warrior and continues his journey.
>
> A few days later he reaches a larger village. In the

center of town is a man of medium build; he is wearing silver robes, and he has a long sword and a small box attached to his sash. "I'm guessing," says the traveler, "but are you the second greatest Samurai in all of Japan?" "I am," says the warrior. "Would you like a demonstration?" The silver warrior opens the top of the box attached to his sash. A fly buzzes out. The fly flits around the warrior's head. He swiftly draws his sword and swings it at the fly. The fly's wings are severed from its body. The fly drops to the ground and crawls away.

A few days later, the traveler reaches Kyoto. As he walks past the many beautiful temples, he sees a large man dressed in gold robes. The man has a long sword and a box attached to his sash. "You must be the greatest Samurai in all of Japan," says the man. "Yes, I am," says the warrior. "Would you like a demonstration?" The warrior opens the top of the box attached to his sash. A fly buzzes out. The fly flits around the warrior's head. He waits. The fly begins to fly away. The warrior whips out his sword and swings it at the fly. The fly flies away, unaffected.

"He flew away!" says the traveler. "Oh, he may fly," says the warrior, "but he'll never fuck again."

[This is another joke that I present dramatically. I indicate the path of the fly with my forefinger, and I go through all the actions of pulling out the sword and swinging at the fly.]

*

A man wakes up one morning and walks into his bathroom. He looks in his mirror and sees a small red pimple in the middle of his forehead. He squeezes it, and an electric pain shoots down his back, dropping him to his knees. As he catches his breath, he thinks to himself, "This can't be good." He calls his doctor and makes an appointment for later in the day.

That afternoon, the man waits for the doctor in the examination room. The doctor walks in, looks at the pimple on the man's forehead, and says, "Holy smoke! I've read about this, but I've never actually seen it."

He examines the pimple under a magnifying glass, and checks several reference books. "What's wrong with me?" asks the man.

"Well, like I say, this isn't very common, and yours is the first case like it I've seen in twenty-five years of practicing medicine. You have a penis growing out of your forehead." "You have got to be kidding me," says the man. "No, I'm serious. In a few months, this will develop into a full size, adult penis."

"Get rid of it then," says the man. "Cut it out." "I can't," says the doctor. "The nerve endings from it go through your brain and attach at the top of your spine. That's why you got the shooting pain down your back when you squeezed it. If we try to remove it you could be paralyzed for life."

"So you're telling me that for the rest of my life, every time I look in the mirror to shave, I'm going to see a big penis coming out of my forehead?"

"Oh no," says the doctor, "the balls will cover your eyes."

*

A piano player is at a recording studio laying down a few tracks. He says to the engineer, "I don't have a lot of time; I have to get over to my restaurant gig. Just start the recorder. I'm going to play three tunes. I'll leave some space between them." The engineer begins recording, and for the next twenty minutes the pianist plays some of the most beautiful music that the engineer has ever heard. After the third tune, the pianist says, "That's it." He puts on his coat and starts to leave.

"Wait a minute," says the engineer. "I need to mark the log sheet with the names of those tunes so I can refer back to them later when we mix." "Okay, says the pianist, "the first tune was called 'I Love You So Fucking Much I Could Shit.' The second tune was called 'Bend Over Baby While I Bang You in the Ass.' The third one is called 'Who Needs You Bitch, I've Got my Dog and a Jar of Peanut Butter.'"

The engineer says, "You have to be kidding me. Those are the most disgusting song titles I've ever heard." The pianist says, "Hey, that's what I was thinking about when I wrote the songs, and those are the titles I gave them. Just log them that way." He leaves the studio.

The pianist arrives at the restaurant, sits down at the piano, and plays for an hour. The music is absolutely beautiful. He gets up and goes to the restroom. As he walks back to the piano, it's obvious to everyone in the room that he has not taken the time to adjust his clothing properly. His genitals are exposed.

He sits down at the piano and begins to play. A man walks up to him and says, "Hey, do you know your cock and balls are lying on the piano bench?"

The pianist says, "Know it? I wrote it!"

[This is the other great cocktail pianist joke I referred to earlier in the book. Robin Williams and Drew Carey do a great tag-team telling of this joke in the movie *The Aristocrats*.]

*

There are two Siamese-twin sisters who live in Laughlin, Nevada. They are in love with Julio Iglesias. When she gets sexually aroused, the sister on the right (that's her right, not your right) has to give oral sex. When the sister on the left (that's her left) gets sexually aroused, she has to play her trombone. These behaviors are compulsive and uncontrollable.

One day, one of the sisters sees in the paper that Julio Iglesias is coming to Harrah's in Laughlin. The sisters immediately purchase tickets, and they count the days until Julio comes to town. On the evening of the concert, the sisters dress in their snazziest outfits; each sister has a rose to offer to Julio during the concert; and, of course, the sister on the left has her trombone. They have front row seats.

The concert is fantastic. Julio walks into the audience and takes the roses from the sisters. After the concert, the sisters go backstage. They explain to Julio's assistant that they are his biggest fans. The assistant lets them into the dressing room.

The sisters start to talk to Julio, but being this close to him is simply too much for the sister on the right. She is aroused beyond her ability to control herself. She drops to her knees, bringing Julio's pants (and her sister) down with her, and starts to give him a frantic blowjob. This pushes the other sister over the edge. She takes out her trombone and starts to play *Tiger Rag*. The sister on the right finishes off Julio in a frenzy of heads, hands, and glissandos.

Eighteen months pass. One sister is reading the newspaper, and she sees that Julio Iglesias is coming back to Harrah's. "Julio is coming back," she tells her sister. "We should go see him again." "That's wonderful," says the other sister. "I wonder if we can go backstage again."

"I don't know," says the first sister. "Do you think he'll remember us?"

[Mac King told me this joke as we were driving to a pet store to buy goldfish for one of the tricks in his show. The joke was new to me, and the punch line really cracked me up. It comes out of nowhere.]

*

A man walks into the emergency room of a hospital. Apparently, he has been cut badly; there is blood streaming down his forearm. [I hold my right forearm in a vertical position with the hand in a fist.] "Holy smoke," says the emergency room receptionist, "what happened to you?" "I was banging my girlfriend, and my wife walked in and caught me. She came at me with a knife."

"You're lucky," says the receptionist. "I would have cut your balls off."

The man goes: [I lower my forearm to a horizontal position and slowly open my fist.]

*

A man is sitting at a bar, nursing a scotch and soda. The bartender says, "You seem a little depressed, pal." "I am," says the man. "I haven't been laid in a long time." "Well," says the bartender, "the gal at the other end of the bar is a working girl. If you have the dough, she'll be happy to take care of you." "I really hate to have to pay for it," says the man, but he finishes his drink and walks to where the hooker sits.

"I understand you're a working girl," he says. "What's the deal?" "Well," she says, "straight sex is five hundred dollars." "Five hundred dollars!" says the man. "Is there anything a little less expensive?"

"A blow job is a hundred and fifty." she says. "That's still a little high," replies the man. "Do you have anything cheaper?"

"For twenty-five dollars I'll give you a 'penguin'," the hooker says. "I'm not familiar with that," says the man. "It's pretty nice," says the hooker.

So, the money changes hands. Almost immediately the man's coat is off and his pants are around his ankles. [Slip your jacket off your shoulders so it hangs down around your waist.] The hooker starts in on him. She is giving him the best blow job he has ever had. She gets him right to the edge, when, all of a sudden, she stands up and walks away.

"Hey," says the man. "Where are you going?" [Waddle forward as if your pants are around your ankles. Since your coat is around your waist, your arms stick out like a penguin's wings.]

[This is one of the best visual jokes I know. Jay Marshall was the first person I saw perform it. For the right group it kills.]

Penn Jillette has said that for a joke to be truly funny it must have talking animals and anal sex. We conclude this section with two jokes that fit those criteria, just in case he's right.

A lion is drinking from a small pond in the middle of the jungle. A chimpanzee sees him, runs over, lifts his tail, and quickly fucks him in the ass. The lion lets out a tremendous roar of anger and surprise. The chimp hops off and races into the jungle with the lion in hot pursuit.

The two dodge and weave through the jungle. The chimp takes to the trees and gains a little distance on the lion. He comes to a clearing where some explorers have set up camp. He runs into a tent, grabs a pith helmet, puts it on, runs outside, hops in a portable canvas chair, picks up a newspaper, and pretends to be reading it.

The lion charges into the clearing. "Roar!" he says. "Did you see a chimpanzee anywhere around here?" From behind the newspaper the chimp says, "Do you mean the chimp that fucked the lion in the ass?"

The lion stops dumbfounded and says, "What, it's in the paper already?"

And last, but certainly not least, one of the greatest jokes ever written.

A biker decides to go bear hunting. He rides out into the countryside, parks his bike, and walks into the woods. He sees a large grizzly bear. He aims and fires. The bear drops and rolls out of sight behind a small hill. The biker walks over to where the bear fell; there's no bear. Just then, there's a tap on the biker's shoulder. It's the bear.

"Basically, you have two options," says the bear. "Option one is that I rip off your head, arms, and legs and I eat your entrails for lunch. Option two is that you suck my dick."

Ten minutes later, the biker is back on his bike, riding home and trying to get the taste of bear out of his mouth. "Goddamn that bear," he thinks. The next day he buys an Uzi and rides back to the woods. He sees the bear and opens fire with the Uzi. Small trees, squirrels, and birds are mowed down. The bear drops and rolls behind a hill. The biker walks over to where the bear fell; there's no bear. Just then, there's a tap on the biker's shoulder. It's the bear.

"Basically, you have two options," says the bear. "Option one is that I rip off your head, arms, and legs and I eat your entrails for lunch. Option two is that I fuck you in the ass."

Twenty minutes later, the biker is painfully riding back to town. "Goddamn that bear," he thinks. The next day, he buys a bazooka and rides back to the woods. It's easy to spot the bear; there's not much foliage left from the day before. He draws a bead on the bear and fires. There's a big explosion. The biker walks over to where the bear fell; there's no bear. Just then, there's a tap on the biker's shoulder. It's the bear.

The bear says, "Be honest. You're not just here for the hunting, are you?"

[This is one of those rare dirty jokes in which the set-up is completely filthy, but the punch line is clean. For this reason, the punch line has shown up on network television programs that normally would not allow such vulgar humor. I remember watching an episode of *Cybil* that dropped in the punch line unexpectedly. I fell off the couch laughing.]

Last Laugh

The chapter you are now reading is not the same chapter that I started to write a few weeks ago. The title, tone, and content were markedly different. As so often happens, I had planned one thing, but life sent me off on a different course. I'll tell you what happened in a moment.

I'm writing this book in Antigua, Guatemala. Lisa and I came down here on February 5, 2007, to take over the foster care of our daughter Ava. Lisa stayed here; I went back to Vegas. I came back for a visit in May, and then returned on July 25, 2007, to wait with my family for our paperwork to clear the Guatemalan adoption bureaucracy. As I write this, we are in the home stretch, but there are still several hoops to jump through before we can go home. The previous eight months have been filled with stress, frustration, anxiety, disappointment, sadness, loneliness, and (when all of us were together in Guatemala) great joy. The concept of this joke book had been rolling around in my head for several years. Working on it here in Antigua seemed like an excellent use of my time, and I launched into the writing with enthusiasm.

Recording these jokes, anecdotes, and personal reminiscences has been a therapeutic act of recollection. I was very surprised at how many jokes came to mind as I started to write. At first, I wrote reminders of the jokes on sticky notes. This quickly became unwieldy, so I kept a small notebook by the computer and jotted down punch lines as they came to me. In a short time, I had recorded well over two hundred jokes. The jokes themselves brought back a flood of memories of people and places, and these memories were filled with laughter. In a foreign country, in a difficult and stressful situation, the ability to call up these happy memories was a great gift. And that, of course, is the purpose of this book, to share this gift with you.

Life is memory. By the time you read this, the writing of this book will be a memory for me. Soon, the reading of this book will be a memory for you. The individual moments of our lives rush by; all we can carry with us are the memories. When rough times show up, it is often the memories of happier times that sustain us.

As I mentioned in the chapter on Chuck Fayne, I came to fatherhood late in life. I turned fifty-five nine days ago. Ava will be one year old in a week. Watching her develop and grow has been a wonderful experience. I am struck by the fact that tears and laughter are hard wired in human beings. As a built-in response, crying makes perfect sense to me. It's our first reaction to pain, hunger, cold, fear, frustration, loss, and every other bad thing that life throws at us. Crying lets everybody else know that something is wrong, and for babies this ability is crucial for survival. Laughter is more curious. Human beings must need it; would it have made the evolutionary cut otherwise? But laughter is tougher to evoke. You have to work for it. Tears are easy. Left to its own devices, nature is going to go for the tears. The way life works, there's nothing very funny about it. Ava can cry at the drop of a hat; if I want laughs from her, I have to pull out the A material.

During the eight months that Lisa and Ava have been together in Guatemala, I've tried to follow Bob Read's example and discover the funny five minutes that I could get out of our situation, but I couldn't find it. Nothing about this long process with all its delays and snafus seemed funny to me. With all we've endured, I thought it unlikely that anything else could go wrong. But it did, and, surprisingly, I found my five minutes.

Two days before my birthday, I was rushed to a hospital here in Antigua. I was suffering from bronchial pneumonia, acute pancreatitis, and several other problems. I was in bad shape; the pain from the pancreatitis was unlike any I had ever experienced. I'm good with pain. I often manage it by mentally moving myself to a happier place (another good reason to have laughter memories in reserve). But because it hurt every time I took a breath (no matter how shallow), I couldn't get away from the pain.

The doctors, nurses, and support staff in the hospital were terrific; I can't say enough good things about them. My case was complex; they handled it with professionalism, dedication, and genuine concern.

I was hooked up to a monitor that kept track of my vital signs. This monitor beeped in response to the rhythm of my heart. These beeps were not fixed pitches; they rose and fell, without any logic that I could discern. The rhythm would speed up or slow down with my heart rate, but every now and then a goofy rhythm would get tossed in. Sometimes this would repeat, sometimes not. Sometimes the pattern was regular, sometimes not. The problem was that, as a musician, I could not help grouping these beeps into weird melodies; I could not push them into the background. The beeps were all I heard. I couldn't sleep. They drove me nuts. I asked everyone who came into the room to shut the sound of the monitor off. No one could.

My room had a TV set mounted high up on the far wall; it received twelve channels, all of them in Spanish. The remote control didn't work. If I wanted a channel changed, or the volume altered, or the TV turned on or off, I had to call for a nurse's aid, who would then climb up on a chair to make the necessary adjustment. With the TV on and the volume cranked up, the beeps from the monitor faded into the background and I could sleep.

Late in the evening on my third day in the hospital, a young doctor came into the room. He was a nice guy, and spoke some English. He examined me and checked on the status of the various bags of fluids that were dripping into me. As he started to leave, he said, "You watch a lot of television." I explained to him that the only reason I had the TV on was to drown out the sound of the monitor so I could sleep. "Oh," he said, "we can shut that sound off." He worked on the monitor for a moment, and the beeping ceased. I couldn't believe it. He hopped up on a chair, shut off the TV, shut off the room lights, and left.

There I was in the dark, and for the first time in three days it was absolutely quiet. I relaxed into my pillow and let out a deep sigh. And then, at the perfect Chuck Jones moment, the machine went, "Beep, beep, beep, beep..." I laughed out loud.

I was in the hospital for six days; I'm much better now, and I'm improving every day. The experience reminded me of another important function of memory – if you pay attention to it, it keeps you from repeating stupid mistakes. I'm going to take better care of myself. I have no desire to go through that experience again.

Until 1990, I had done very little traveling outside of the United States. That year, I began publishing books for magicians. They were well received, and the notoriety I gained from them brought invitations to lecture to magicians around the world. I found myself in a situation I had not encountered before – I was laughing and having fun with people who I probably would never see again.

This was the time when I began to see life as a series of entrances and exits. (Unlike Billy McComb, I try to wrap up a conversation before launching into a new one.) It is also the time when I began saying, "I'll see you down the road," rather than "goodbye." This may be an overly optimistic view of the life process, but it expresses the hope that this parting, no matter how long it may be, is only temporary. Let's face it, all of us are on this journey alone. Occasionally, someone will walk it with us, often for long periods. Other people dart in and out; others we meet only once. Some leave unexpectedly. What we carry with us are the memories of these encounters, and I think it is important that these memories, if possible, be filled with laughter.

That Reminds Me is a book about storytelling, an art form that's rapidly disappearing. Comedy clubs want a laugh every forty-five seconds. We get our news in sound bites. Instead of talking, we text each other. The music in our clubs drowns out the possibility of conversation. Our computers put us in touch with thousands of people around the world, but we hold them safely at arm's length. In spite of all our high-tech connectivity, our society is becoming increasingly isolated. In the face-to-face sharing of stories, however, we reaffirm our humanity, reinforce our similarities rather than our differences, and build the type of memories that can be put in the bank for an emotionally rainy day.

I hope you laughed as you read this book; if so, I'm happy to have done my job well. But the jokes are not meant to be read; they're meant to be told. My wish is for you is to take these jokes and bring them to life by sharing them with your friends. Find an occasion (or better yet, make an occasion) to spend time with your pals and create some laughter-filled memories. (Remember one of the key adages of show business: leave them wanting more. You have a huge arsenal of material available to you; dole it out in small chunks.)

I'd also be pleased if you shared the stories about the people you met in this book. One of the things I miss most about Jay Marshall and Billy McComb is their stories. They told me about people who were no longer around, people I would never have the chance to meet, and in the telling of those stories they brought those people to life. The stories you tell will do the same for the people in your life.

And most important, always be looking for the "Bob Read five minutes" in whatever situation you find yourself. Life is tough. Life wants tears. Fight back; look hard and try to find the funny. I think this is one of most important things I can teach my daughter. Fortunately, she has a head start. As I mentioned in the Dedication, she has a great laugh.